A SHOT IN THE DARK

A Shot in the Dark

A new comedy

Adapted by Harry Kurnitz

From *L'Idiote* by Marcel Achard

Random House, New York

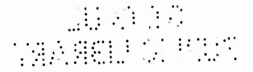

To M. Y. Calisto

A Shot in the Dark *was first presented by Leland Hayward at the Booth Theatre, New York City, on October 18, 1961, with the following cast:*

(IN ORDER OF APPEARANCE)

Paul Sevigne	William Shatner
Morestan	Gene Saks
Lablache	Hugh Franklin
Antoinette Sevigne	Diana van der Vlis
Josefa Lantenay	Julie Harris
Guard	Pierre Epstein
Dominique Beaurevers	Louise Troy
Benjamin Beaurevers	Walter Matthau

Directed by Harold Clurman

Setting and lighting by Ben Edwards

Costumes by Noel Taylor

SYNOPSIS OF SCENES

Act One

Early afternoon in December. The time is the present.

Act Two

Early afternoon, two days later.

Act Three

The same day, late afternoon.

All the action of the play takes place in the chambers of an Examining Magistrate (*juge d'instruction*) in an old municipal building in Paris. It is quite a large room with an air of seedy, run-down grandeur still persisting in the domed, painted ceiling, on which cherubs and peeling plaster are intermingled; tapestry covers the walls, some of this also reasonably shredded through the years; there is a chipped and battered—but still elegant—chandelier. The furnishings are abundant and varied, ranging from quite a good writing table, which is the desk of the Magistrate, to some cheap modern filing cabinets in which repose the records of Justice. Another ordinary table, covered with a cloth, serves as the desk of the Clerk and this is arranged so that the two functionaries face each other and are separated by almost the width of the room. A straight chair between the two desks is reserved for witnesses and there are a couple of other chairs, of varying styles and periods, scattered around the room. A bookcase, behind the Magistrate's desk, holds his law library, and a good many of the books are now scattered—open and closed—on his desk. There are double doors at the center of the stage, which are used for nearly all entrances and exits, but there is also a door at the left which leads to a small adjoining room in which certain witnesses can be asked to wait.

ACT ONE

sc. 11

At rise, the Magistrate, PAUL SEVIGNE, is alone. He is seated at his desk, immersed in lawbooks and the contents of a large loose-leaf file. He is about thirty-five and at the moment he is wearing horn-rimmed glasses, which he uses for reading. They give him a scholarly air which tends to recede when he takes them off. He is a good-looking young man and well dressed in a careful, sober way.

The Clerk, MORESTAN, enters. He is young—about SEVIGNE's age, in fact—but already hardened and cynical by his years in the service.

MORESTAN What a lunch! Believe me, you were wise to stay here and work! (*He hangs his hat and coat on a coat rack*) Restaurants in Paris these days! The odds are worse than in the National Lottery. (*He removes his shoes, putting on slippers, then bangs the shoes into a file cabinet apparently reserved for this purpose. He sees that SEVIGNE is still deep in his researches and he shakes his head pityingly*) Still at the lawbooks?

SEVIGNE (*Apologetically*) It's my first case—a murder.

MORESTAN Murder! *That's* not the point. A case is a case. The police have handed you a suspect, haven't they?

SEVIGNE Yes . . . the maid.

MORESTAN All right. Fire a few questions at her, get her to sign a statement, then you clap her into prison and get on to something else.

SEVIGNE Is that how it's done?

3

MORESTAN Sure! I've worked on dozens of these. Believe me, it's the best way.

SEVIGNE What about this? (*He picks up one of the open law-books, reads*) "An accused person must be protected from any infringement of his or her rights under the law . . . from the police or from the law itself . . . this is the first and the most sacred obligation of an examining magistrate."
(*He glances up at* MORESTAN, *replacing the book*)

MORESTAN (*With a sigh*) Well, if you believe everything you read . . . (*With a helpless gesture*) Let's have a look at the summary of the evidence from the police.

SEVIGNE Sure . . . right here . . .
(*He fumbles in his file for the appropriate paper*)

MORESTAN (*Pained*) In an interrogation, don't fumble for papers like that. The witness may get the idea that you're not sure of yourself. Here—let me show you. (SEVIGNE *surrenders the file,* MORESTAN *demonstrates*) Locate the document in advance, keep your finger on it, then *whip* it out!
(*Which he does with a flourish*)

SEVIGNE (*Intrigued*) That's not bad . . . let me try that . . .
(*He takes the file from* MORESTAN)

MORESTAN I'm the witness . . . (*Seating himself in the chair*) Go on—give me the works. Don't spare me! (SEVIGNE, *holding the file, is already circling the chair with a panther tread.* MORESTAN *nods approvingly*) Very nice!

SEVIGNE Did you know that a loaded revolver was kept in the Rolls-Royce?

MORESTAN (*Cringing*) No . . . I didn't know that.

4

SEVIGNE   Ah! I intend to refresh your memory. (*He has located the document, now whips it out with such a flourish that the paper flies out of his hand, to the floor*) Oh, hell!

MORESTAN   Don't worry; it takes a bit of practice, that's all. (*Retrieving the paper*)

SEVIGNE   I'd better stick to my books and what I know.

MORESTAN   No, you'll be fine—(*He glances at the paper in his hand*) Say, the girl was found naked?

SEVIGNE   Yes—she fainted after the shooting, still holding the weapon. The chauffeur was her lover, they quarreled violently, she shot him. (*Thoughtfully*) There seems to be quite a bit of that in Paris.

MORESTAN   Only in the winter—people are cooped up together. Ah, he beat her up now and then, eh?

SEVIGNE   Yes, once too often, apparently.

MORESTAN   Well, there you are—a snap, nothing to it—practically tied up in blue ribbons for you.
(MONSIEUR LABLACHE *enters at center. He is the Deputy Chief Prosecutor, a smartly turned-out bureaucrat in black coat and striped trousers, also wearing an air of casual authority*)

LABLACHE   (*Cheerfully*)   Good afternoon, Sevigne . . . Morestan . . .

MORESTAN   Good afternoon, Monsieur Lablache.

LABLACHE   I thought I'd stop by to see how you were getting on . . . Your first interrogation today, isn't it?

SEVIGNE   Yes . . . in a few minutes, in fact.

LABLACHE It's that shooting in the rue de la Faisanderie, isn't it? The maid and the chauffeur making love in her room ... outbursts of jealousy, and—bang! (*Shrugs philosophically*) Well, can't expect them to watch television forever. (*Reaches for the file*) Is this it? (*As* SEVIGNE *nods*) May I? (*Takes the file, seats himself, glancing through it*) Ah! Splendid! (*He beams with obvious and great pleasure*) The maid was found on the scene of the crime ... the murder weapon in her hand ... *very* nice! (*Drops the file casually on* SEVIGNE's *desk*) Congratulations, Sevigne! An open-and-shut case.

SEVIGNE (*Uncomfortably*) Well, *her* story is that the door opened behind them, a shot was fired in the dark, and she promptly fainted.

LABLACHE *That's* her story? Well, warn her that if she sticks to that, she'll be guilty of murder *and* contempt of court! Really! (*Meaningfully*) By the way, that's not just my opinion—that's how the Chief Prosecutor sees it, too.

SEVIGNE (*Surprised*) The Chief Prosecutor? Has *he* followed the investigation?

LABLACHE Are you mad? Certainly not! Do you honestly expect the Chief Prosecutor to concern himself with the case of a parlormaid and a chauffeur bouncing from bed to bed until one of them died from it?

SEVIGNE I just don't see how the Chief could form this opinion, unless he—

LABLACHE (*Pointedly*) The girl and her victim both worked in the household of Benjamin Beaurevers.

SEVIGNE That's a bank, isn't it?

LABLACHE Yes, a bank. Tell him, Morestan.

A SHOT IN THE DARK

MORESTAN   In Paris, *the* bank. Beaurevers Frères! Billions!

LABLACHE   And a fine old family! (*Respectfully*) Before her marriage, she was a St. Maur de Pignarolles!

MORESTAN   A member of the Beaurevers family rode beside the King in the First Crusade!

LABLACHE   Just so. He was, in fact, the treasurer.

SEVIGNE   I see what you mean . . .

LABLACHE   Of course you do! Get a confession from the girl—a short one, if possible, and you'll be home in time for an early dinner. Good luck, Sevigne. Call me the moment you've disposed of the case and I'll pass the good news along—to the top.

(*With a nod to* MORESTAN, *he goes*)

SEVIGNE   You know, Morestan, the Beaurevers family must be very nice, kind people. After all, they could have tried the girl themselves, found her guilty and guillotined her in the kitchen without consulting anybody.

MORESTAN   The rich like things done their way. Otherwise, what would be the point of having all that money?

SEVIGNE (*Slamming a book*)   Damn!

MORESTAN   I know how you feel. But what's the harm? The girl is guilty, isn't she?

SEVIGNE   What if she is? She should be tried by a judge and a jury, not by the social register and a bank!

MORESTAN   You're taking it too seriously. This is a business, and it's the Chief Prosecutor who runs it—now just think along those lines—(*He is interrupted by the entrance of* ANTOINETTE SEVIGNE. *Antoinette is young, bright, very pretty,*

7

the wife of the disgruntled Magistrate. She is dressed with modest chic. MORESTAN, *rising*) Oh, good afternoon, Madame Sevigne.

ANTOINETTE   Hello, Monsieur Morestan.

SEVIGNE   Hello, Antoinette—come on in.
   (*His greeting is cheerless and she looks at him anxiously*)

ANTOINETTE   You don't mind. I'm not interrupting something important?

SEVIGNE   No . . . I've just been having a law lesson—from the Chief Prosecutor.

MORESTAN (*Tactfully*)   Why don't I slip out and get a notebook you'll need.
   (*He exits*)

ANTOINETTE   Darling, what's wrong?

SEVIGNE   Nothing—now.
   (*He gives her a bit smile*)

ANTOINETTE   You're not angry with me for coming here?

SEVIGNE   You arrived in the nick of time.

ANTOINETTE   Your first case . . . I wanted to wish you good luck.
   (*She embraces him—warmly*)

SEVIGNE   Antoinette!

ANTOINETTE (*Holding on*)   Well, I need *something* to take my mind off apartment-hunting.

SEVIGNE   Read a good book or take a cold shower.

ANTOINETTE If you knew the kind of places I've seen: dark, dirty halls; dingy little rooms—and we can't even afford those.

SEVIGNE Paris is for tourists. In Lyons we had a beautiful apartment. Modern, sunny, all conveniences—

ANTOINETTE *What* conveniences? It was three hundred miles from Christian Dior.

SEVIGNE There was that drawback.

ANTOINETTE Darling, the best possible incentive to success for any young magistrate is an extravagant young wife.

SEVIGNE That's not a law—only a rumor.

ANTOINETTE I've been right so far, haven't I? Didn't I tell you that within a year we would be out of Lyons, and in Paris?

SEVIGNE Homeless, but closer to Christian Dior. Antoinette, what if I were no good here—and they shipped me back to the law library and my old job?

ANTOINETTE Oh, Paul—no!

SEVIGNE They might.

ANTOINETTE Paul, what's wrong? What's worrying you?

SEVIGNE I don't know. I'm not sure that I fit in here. They seem to do things differently in Paris.

ANTOINETTE Oh, darling!
(*She embraces him*)

SEVIGNE Well, not *those* things.

ANTOINETTE It's just that you're new here ... but you won't be for long. And you're a brilliant lawyer.

SEVIGNE I'm not sure that's enough.

ANTOINETTE It is for me.

SEVIGNE I'm glad you dropped in. I needed you. (*He kisses her. They are separated by a knock*) Come in! (MORESTAN *enters, with a notebook which he will put on* SEVIGNE's *desk*) Morestan, this is your office just as much as it is mine. There is no need for you to knock before entering.

MORESTAN Thank you. You've cut yourself?

SEVIGNE Eh?

ANTOINETTE (*Sotto voce*) Lipstick.
(*She smiles unconcernedly at* MORESTAN *as* SEVIGNE, *embarrassed, dabs at his mouth with a pocket handkerchief*)

MORESTAN It's just about time for our first witness . . .

SEVIGNE Yes. Now, out you go, Antoinette. Find us a nice apartment; ten rooms, four baths, a terrace—and for very little money. That's an order.

ANTOINETTE Yes, sir. Goodbye, Monsieur Morestan . . . goodbye, Paul . . .
(*She blows him a kiss, exits*)

MORESTAN (*Shrewdly*) Feeling better?

SEVIGNE Yes . . . quite a bit.

MORESTAN (*With a shrug*) My wife depresses me. (*Gets up*) Shall I see if the girl is here?

SEVIGNE Yes, let's have her in. (*As* MORESTAN *starts for the door*) What do you think, Morestan—the friendly, fatherly approach for this one?

10

MORESTAN The silent treatment. Let her sweat for a bit. Chances are she'll break down and confess before you ask the first question.

SEVIGNE Then by all means, the silent treatment.

(He buries himself in writing at his desk, first donning his reading glasses. MORESTAN *opens the door.* JOSEFA *is seen sitting on a bench.* MORESTAN *beckons, she rises and enters.* JOSEFA *is very pretty, delicate-looking as one would not expect in one who until recently was a farm girl. Her manner and speech are candid, never common or vulgar, though her voice is not educated or affected.* MORESTAN *points to the chair, and she sits down. She tugs modestly at her skirt, but it is much too short. She glances at* SEVIGNE, *who is bent over his work, utterly ignoring her, then at* MORESTAN, *who is similarly occupied. There is a long silence, while she looks around. Whatever the silent treatment is supposed to effect,* JOSEFA *is apparently totally unimpressed. She takes a package of cigarettes from her purse, extracts one, then fumbles about for a packet of matches. She finds it, strikes one, is just about to touch it to her cigarette)*

MORESTAN *(A bark)* No smoking!

(Startled, JOSEFA *waves out the match, then with a patient, good-humored shrug, she puts away the cigarette, still holding the burnt-out match. She looks around for some place to get rid of this, still utterly ignored by the two men, who are apparently deeply absorbed in their work. Finally, she puts the match in her purse too. The silence is heavy, prolonged)*

JOSEFA Was it for today—I can easily come back tomorrow—
(MORESTAN looks up at her, a long, pitying look, then goes

back to his work. Again the silence. She looks from one to the other, getting no sign of recognition. JOSEFA, *chuckling*) The guard out there told me a funny joke. Two old maids own a drugstore—(*She happens to be looking at* SEVIGNE; *he raises his head and gives her such a long, bleak look that* JOSEFA *stops short.* SEVIGNE *puts his head down over his work again. The silence again. Then* JOSEFA *smiles, as if at last understanding something*) Oh, we're waiting for the Magistrate, is that it?

(SEVIGNE *heaves a deep sigh. The silent treatment is apparently having more effect on him than on its intended "victim," and he abandons the gambit*)

SEVIGNE   I am the Magistrate.

JOSEFA   You? (*She looks at* SEVIGNE *carefully, then just as appraisingly at* MORESTAN, *then shrugs in casual agreement*) All right. (*And as* SEVIGNE *is about to speak*) You don't look it. He's more the type.

(*She indicates* MORESTAN)

SEVIGNE   You'll have to take my word for it.

JOSEFA   I didn't say it to hurt your feelings. I only—

SEVIGNE   Be still! (JOSEFA *clams up. Behind her back* MORESTAN *makes a cautionary gesture.* SEVIGNE *gets a good grip on himself, proceeds quietly*) Your name, please.

JOSEFA   Josefa Lantenay.

SEVIGNE   Where were you born?

JOSEFA   Espoletto—in the province of Drôme.

SEVIGNE   Your age?

JOSEFA   Twenty-four. As a rule, I don't look it, but these last two days—

SEVIGNE (*Interrupting her*) Your occupation?

JOSEFA Parlormaid. (*Glancing around*) Incidentally, your office is filthy. (*As* SEVIGNE *exhales sharply in exasperation*) It is. You should speak to the charwoman. I'm a parlormaid myself, so I know how easy it is to sweep under the rug or—

SEVIGNE Don't wander from the question!

JOSEFA Oh—sorry! (*But she is irrepressible*) It's not healthy to work where there's a lot of dust flying around—
(SEVIGNE's *stare quiets her*)

SEVIGNE (*Rising*) Josefa Lantenay, I am charged by law, as an Examining Magistrate, for the Higher Court, to conduct an enquiry into the death by shooting of one Miguel Ostos.
(*Before he can breathe and continue*)

JOSEFA Poor Miguel! I can hardly believe it. He was so alive and—

SEVIGNE *Furthermore!* (*And as she subsides*) Furthermore, I am empowered to examine witnesses and accused persons in this affair, to interrogate them, and, if necessary to confront them with each other. My findings may be a basis for the arrest and imprisonment of any person or persons sufficiently implicated, and my recommendations will guide the presiding judge of any subsequent trial. Do you understand?

JOSEFA (*Cheerfully*) I am innocent.

SEVIGNE I didn't ask you that!

JOSEFA I thought I'd tell you—to save you the trouble of questioning me.

SEVIGNE It's no trouble, I assure you.

JOSEFA All right. Shall I tell you what happened, in my own words?

SEVIGNE Certainly not! (JOSEFA *shrugs as if it was all too much for her but she is willing to go along.* SEVIGNE *has a momentary struggle to maintain his judicial calm*) Above all, Josefa Lantenay, be absolutely truthful in replying to my questions. If you tell even the slightest lie—

JOSEFA Why should I lie? I have nothing to fear. (*Chattily*) As my father used to say, if you're poor, there are two worries you *don't* have—pickpockets, and lawyers.

(MORESTAN *chokes back a laugh.* SEVIGNE *looks at him grimly, then at* JOSEFA)

JOSEFA (*Contrite*) I'm sorry. You're a lawyer, aren't you?

SEVIGNE Don't you also want to know if I'm a pickpocket?

JOSEFA I'm sorry. (SEVIGNE *turns back to the desk, glancing at one of the lawbooks open there, refreshing his grip on the technique, also giving himself an opportunity to get the questioning under control. When he turns back to* JOSEFA, *he is composed again.* JOSEFA, *before he can speak*) I'm sorry about what I said—

SEVIGNE All right!

JOSEFA I didn't mean to be fresh, or—

SEVIGNE All right! (*She quiets down. He hesitates, in case she is going to blurt out something, but she waits quietly. The coast is clear*) Are your parents living?

JOSEFA My father, yes. My mother . . . ? (*She shrugs*) I don't know. I never knew her, or anything about her. Strange, isn't it? Generally it is the father one can't identify. (*She is serenely unaware of* SEVIGNE's *impatience*) Four days after I was born, my mother ran away with a railroad conductor. I guess I didn't make a very good impression.

SEVIGNE Your father is a farmer—correct?

JOSEFA And a winegrower. I worked for him until Madame Beaurevers hired me. My father's vineyard was only two kilometers from their chateau. I was their parlormaid for two summers before I came to Paris.

SEVIGNE The deceased, Miguel Ostos, was already in their employ?

JOSEFA Yes—chauffeur. (*Warmly*) In his uniform, *he* was something. Poor Miguel! You know something—at first he didn't appeal to me at all.

SEVIGNE Judging from what you were wearing at the time of the shooting, I'd say that feeling wore off.
    (JOSEFA *tugs modestly at her short skirt, an instinctive gesture, and looks reproachfully at* SEVIGNE)

JOSEFA If you think I *liked* being found that way!

SEVIGNE How long before you changed your mind about Ostos?

JOSEFA Not long . . . I didn't even know it was happening, suddenly I was in love.

SEVIGNE In love? With the man who raped you?

JOSEFA (*Startled*) Who—*what?*
    (SEVIGNE *has flicked a paper out of the file deftly.* MORESTAN *gives him an applauding look*)

SEVIGNE (*Reading, crisply*) Testimony of Emile Brémontier, janitor. Referring to Ostos, you described him as—and I quote: "that crazy Spaniard who raped me in my father's fields."

JOSEFA (*Thinking*) Actually, it was on the way home from there—(*And then, plaintively*) Say, what have you got in that book?

SEVIGNE On the way home from there? Then he did rape you?

JOSEFA Well . . . rape . . . I wouldn't want to make any trouble for Miguel *now*—

SEVIGNE Is the witness lying? (*Rattling the paper*) Did you say that?

JOSEFA I might have been mad at Miguel that day.

SEVIGNE Will you please answer—yes or no?

JOSEFA Is it important?

SEVIGNE Surely you're the best judge of that. But since it seems to confuse you, let it pass. This should be simpler: when you met Ostos, were you a virgin?

JOSEFA (*Startled*) What's being investigated here? I mean, justice is one thing, but—

SEVIGNE Answer!

JOSEFA My *father* never even asked me such a question!

SEVIGNE A few days in jail will make you more cooperative. Morestan, get the guard—
    (*As* MORESTAN *is about to rise*)

JOSEFA No. Don't. (*Sulking, though*) Some questions! You're sure you're the judge? (*Turning to* MORESTAN) Is he really—

16

SEVIGNE Morestan—the guard—

JOSEFA No, no—please—I'll tell you. (*She takes a breath*) Well— This is all confidential, isn't it? (*And at* SEVIGNE's *mounting impatience*) All right, all right. What was it again —did he rape me, or—

SEVIGNE Read the question, Morestan, please.

MORESTAN (*Reading*) When you met Ostos, were you a virgin?

JOSEFA Ah, yes, of course.

SEVIGNE You mean, you were?

JOSEFA I mean, I remember the question.

SEVIGNE Once and for all, will you answer it?

JOSEFA All right. You're in such a hurry to know, you'd think we were engaged. (*And then*) You know how it is in the provinces . . . boys and girls working side by side in the fields or the vineyards all summer . . . cooling off with a swim now and then . . . getting warm from the work . . . nobody wears very much . . . (*Her fear and antagonism forgotten, she gives* SEVIGNE *a warm, sunny smile*) You'd like Espoletto!

SEVIGNE I don't doubt it.

JOSEFA Don't go in July—it rains quite a lot.

SEVIGNE Now, then, you and the deceased, Ostos.

JOSEFA (*pained*) You make him sound so very *dead!*

SEVIGNE Correction. You and Miguel Ostos. When? Why? How?

JOSEFA When? Why? How? (*Ruefully*) I guess I'm lucky you don't want pictures. (*Then quickly, at* SEVIGNE's *impa-*

tient look) All right, I'm telling. It was in August, the second or third Wednesday, I'm sure it was Wednesday, because we both had the day off. (*Reminiscently*) The heat was awful that day but at sundown it was better. We walked to the vineyard to say hello to my father, then back along the river. The animals were being driven in from the fields . . . there was a sort of a haze over everything along the river bank . . .

SEVIGNE Please! I see the scene very clearly.

JOSEFA I want you to understand how it happened.

SEVIGNE I'll understand. Just tell me what happened.

JOSEFA I tripped over a root. I grabbed Miguel to keep from falling and somehow we both fell.
    (SEVIGNE *waits for more, but there isn't any more*)

SEVIGNE As simply as that?

JOSEFA It was our day off. (*And then delicately*) The heat, you know, and to tell you the truth, I wasn't wearing very much. I mean, underneath. (MORESTAN, *intrigued, has stopped writing altogether. A look from* SEVIGNE *sends him back to his notes*) Anyway, there we were, Miguel and I . . . (SEVIGNE *seems to be waiting*) Doesn't that give you the general idea?

SEVIGNE You didn't fight him off? You put up no resistance?

JOSEFA In that heat? (*Then warmly*) I cried a little bit afterwards, but that wasn't because I was sorry it happened. It was something Miguel said that broke me up. He lit a cigarette, took a long puff—(*Suddenly, irrelevantly*) Why do so many men smoke afterwards? Anyway, Miguel lit a cigarette, took a long puff, and then he said: "Long live the mother who made you!" I fell in love with him right then and there.

SEVIGNE (*Formally*) I should point out to you—if Miguel Ostos did overpower you and force his attentions on you, that might appear as an extenuating circumstance in your favor.

JOSEFA Forced his attentions on me. I like that. That's a nice way to put it. (*And then, suspiciously*) Say, why do I need extenuating circumstances?

SEVIGNE One never knows—they come in handy.

JOSEFA You don't think I did it, do you?

SEVIGNE I have not formed an opinion.

JOSEFA (*Relieved*) Oh.

SEVIGNE However, if you're found with a gun in your hand, and there's a body on the floor . . .
(*He shrugs, letting her form her own conclusions*)

JOSEFA But I *liked* Miguel. You believe that, don't you? *Please* believe that much.

SEVIGNE All right.

JOSEFA Thank you. (SEVIGNE *turns to his desk, darting a quick look at one of the lawbooks.* JOSEFA, *meanwhile, addresses* MORESTAN) He's nice. (MORESTAN *gives her a stern look. She turns back to* SEVIGNE *who crosses to her, file in hand. She makes a face*) Oh-oh! That book again!

SEVIGNE Ostos talked of suicide, didn't he?

JOSEFA Spaniards. They talk.

SEVIGNE You didn't think he meant it?

JOSEFA   Him—suicide? A man who used to cross himself before he made love? (*In her confiding manner*) Oh, I never mentioned it to him. I mean, who knows what people are really thinking at a time like that. Me for instance, I always pretend I'm on the deck of a big sailboat with seagulls flapping all around. Or sometimes that I'm on top of a big mountain, above the clouds—(JOSEFA, *rambling on contentedly, becomes aware of* SEVIGNE's *grim look. She dries up*) Oh—you're not interested?

SEVIGNE   If you go on like this, we'll be here all night.

JOSEFA   Just *us?*

SEVIGNE   Just *you.* Answer the questions. Don't keep wandering from the point.

JOSEFA   Yes, sir.

SEVIGNE   He beat you, didn't he?

JOSEFA   Well—you know—we were in love.

SEVIGNE   That's why he beat you?

JOSEFA   (*Proudly*)   Never when he was drinking!

SEVIGNE   Witnesses have testified that in September and October you exhibited bruises on your face, arms and body—marks of beatings given you by Miguel Ostos.

JOSEFA   It was just in a conversation . . . one brags a little.

SEVIGNE   You quarreled bitterly. (*As she is about to speak*) Don't deny it! (*Tapping the file*) Here is the testimony of neighbors who swear that your fighting disturbed their sleep.

JOSEFA   Ha!

SEVIGNE   What sort of answer is that?

JOSEFA Neighbors! Our fighting didn't bother them. What disturbed their sleep was when we made up. (*A tender memory*) Ah, Miguel, Miguel! He had a terrible temper but he certainly didn't hold a grudge.

SEVIGNE In any event, your relationship was continuously violent—do you deny that?

JOSEFA What else could it be? He was a Spaniard. He'd sit half the night at the window, sometimes, without speaking a single word, then throw himself on me, tearing at my clothes. It was a great nuisance, I promise you, because sometimes he'd just tear and rip every which way, and I hate sewing. (*Chattily*) Strange, isn't it? Housework, cooking, I love all that, but for some reason, I detest sewing. (*Sensing his impatience*) Oh, I'm sorry. You're getting annoyed with me.

SEVIGNE If you would just avoid wandering from the facts, please.

JOSEFA I knew it. I could tell from the look on your face. How often I'd see that same expression on Miguel, and the next minute, he'd clout me one.

SEVIGNE It's a temptation.

JOSEFA No . . . you're not the type.

SEVIGNE You're very perceptive.

JOSEFA One learns about men—from men. (*And then, with a deep sigh*) Poor Miguel! He had only two passions in his life—(*After a pause*) The other was bullfights.

SEVIGNE From time to time he seems to have gotten the two confused.

JOSEFA Poor Miguel! You should have seen his room—bull-fight posters and souvenirs all over the place. He even took a Spanish paper, for the reviews. Poor Miguel! Just last week he was all worked up about a *corrida* in Mexico City. (*She leans forward excitedly, one aficionado to another*) Luis Miguel Dominguín, with Rodrigo bulls—the most dangerous breed—horns like sabres! Dominguín made the first few passes kneeling in front of the *barrera,* and he himself planted the *banderillas.* Then a great *faena,* and what a kill! A single thrust of the sword—to the hilt. The crowd went mad and the judges gave him *both* ears, the tail, and one hoof. Even in Mexico, that's a lot. (*In a small voice, cheering*) Ole! Dominguín! Ole!

(*Then to* SEVIGNE'S *amazement, she bursts into tears.* MORESTAN *looks up from his writing, the two men regard each other helplessly*)

SEVIGNE Oh, God! (*As* JOSEFA *sobs on*) How did we get to this?

(MORESTAN *gives her the silent treatment*)

SEVIGNE (*Roughly*) Blow your nose!
(*He is touched, though*)

JOSEFA (*Sniffling*) I haven't got a handkerchief.

SEVIGNE Here.
(*Gives her his handkerchief*)

JOSEFA Thank you. I hate to cry. Excuse me.

SEVIGNE Go right ahead. (*He uses the interlude to turn back to his desk for a refresher course in criminal law, shaking his head, discouraged. Then he turns back*) Better now?

JOSEFA   Yes. I'm sorry. It was just . . . thinking about Miguel —(*Wistfully*) Do you think—wherever he is *now*—there are bullfights?

SEVIGNE   (*Startled*)   Bullfights? I don't know . . . maybe.

JOSEFA   Well—maybe at least a Spanish paper, with reviews. (*Offering* SEVIGNE *the handkerchief*) I'm fine now. I won't do it again.

SEVIGNE   Keep it . . . you never can tell.

JOSEFA   No. I'm fine now. I won't need the handkerchief— (*Extending it to him*) I promise you.

SEVIGNE   (*Ignoring the handkerchief*)   You knew Ostos wanted to get married? (*As she nods*) To someone else?

JOSEFA   He got ambitious suddenly. This girl, her parents are rich—they own a butcher shop.

SEVIGNE   You weren't jealous?

JOSEFA   Of her father's money? A butcher shop, in a good location, that's something. And *my* dowry—(*She laughs*) My father didn't know about me and Miguel until I was in Paris. Then he sent me a wire: "*Don't* come home and all is forgiven." Funny old Pop—

SEVIGNE   Love or money, you knew Ostos would leave you?

JOSEFA   What could I do about it? (*Then, incredulously*) You don't think that gave me a reason for killing Miguel?

SEVIGNE   (*Mildly*)   It happens, you know . . . a woman scorned . . .

JOSEFA   You've got it all wrong. I kept reminding him about the money and telling him she was beautiful—(*Confidentially*) Beautiful: Just between us, a real dog.

23

SEVIGNE So you were reconciled to losing him? It didn't bother you?

JOSEFA What lasts forever?

SEVIGNE Yet he died in your room . . . you were nude.

JOSEFA Please! (*Tugging at her skirt*) I'll tell you about that —it was to be the last time. His idea, not mine, but I thought, well, so what? Why not part friends? I mean, after all, I *liked* him.

SEVIGNE Apparently.

JOSEFA Poor Miguel! He was really in one of his moods. First he babbled in Spanish, then he cried—really broke down and cried—and when I tried to console him, make him feel better, (*Spanish oath*) suddenly he was tearing off my clothes, throwing them all around the room and cursing like a madman. Believe me, it's a good thing I wanted to part friends, or I would have belted him with an ash tray. I hate that kind of hurly-burly. After all, it's not something you do for exercise, is it?

SEVIGNE Strange, isn't it? Ostos was leaving *you,* and by your own account, *he* was behaving like a jealous madman?

JOSEFA Oh? (*She is slightly apprehensive*) Well—he was funny in a lot of ways . . .
(*She is off balance, though, if only momentarily*)

SEVIGNE Why was he jealous?

JOSEFA I don't know.

SEVIGNE Did he have reason to be?

JOSEFA I don't know. A Spaniard, who knows why he was jealous?

SEVIGNE Then he was?

JOSEFA (*Rattled*) It was foolish—I shouldn't have told him—

SEVIGNE (*Hammering at her*) Told him what?

JOSEFA Poor Miguel! (*She is thinking hard*) I told you I liked him, didn't I?

SEVIGNE Yes—repeatedly.

JOSEFA Well—I thought if he was leaving me, he'd suffer— thinking I was alone—so, I told him there was someone else. It was a lie, I admit that—but, out of kindness.

SEVIGNE Just to make him feel better. There was no other man?

JOSEFA (*Dramatically*) How could there be? When I give my heart—(*She strikes the palm of her hand with her clenched fist*) I give it all! To the hilt!

SEVIGNE You were so considerate? Even though he was going to marry Solange Duval?

JOSEFA Solange! Only a butcher would name his daughter So- lange!

SEVIGNE (*Categorically*) Ostos and the Duval girl went out together—*once*. He took her to the movies and she was hope- lessly bored because all through the film he talked about you. And of his insane jealousy.

JOSEFA Liars—all of them—test the scales in their butcher shop and you'll see what I mean.

SEVIGNE Why was Ostos raving about his jealousy—of whom was he jealous?

JOSEFA I don't know—(*She is getting cornered*) A crazy Spaniard ... he was jealous of shadows.

SEVIGNE (*Formally*) I confront you now with the testimony of Madame Marthe Herbeux.
(*He takes a paper from the file*)

JOSEFA Who?

SEVIGNE The Beaurevers' cook.

JOSEFA Oh, Camel-face.

SEVIGNE Madame Herbeux, interrogated by Inspector Colas, of the police.
Question: "Was Miguel Ostos jealous of Josefa Lantenay?"
Answer: "He was foaming like a fire extinguisher."
Question: "Why?"
Answer: "He knew Josefa was unfaithful to him, but he didn't know with whom."
Question: "Did he suspect one man, or many?"

JOSEFA (*Outraged*) What?

SEVIGNE Be still—
Answer: "One man. Josefa isn't really a whore—just bed-minded!"

JOSEFA Well, at last—a kind word.

SEVIGNE And finally this, from Madame Herbeux: "Only two days before he died, Miguel came raging into my kitchen. He swore he would get the name of the man Josefa was sleeping with, and then—boom! boom!—it would be over quickly. (*Snaps the file shut ominously*) The fact is, Miguel Ostos never dreamed of leaving you. You urged the butcher's daughter on Miguel Ostos because *you* were leaving *him*—had actually left him.

26

JOSEFA He died in my room. And you're forgetting how I was dressed.

SEVIGNE I'll get to that. The cook testifies that Ostos complained for six weeks that your door was locked to him.

JOSEFA Between the book and the cook you'll drive me out of my mind.

SEVIGNE All right. (*He puts the file behind him on the desk.* JOSEFA *is wary now*) The fact is, you had no reason to invent a lover—he existed. You discarded Miguel Ostos for another man.

JOSEFA (*A hint of scorn*) So *that's* what you're investigating?

SEVIGNE Is it true?

JOSEFA (*Evasively*) If I tell you, it all goes in that damned book. I didn't mind coming here—I thought you suspected me of killing Miguel—I mean, after all, that's at least a crime. But all you ask me is what I did where—how—when—with who?

SEVIGNE No more digressions! Is it true? Yes or no?

JOSEFA (*Defiantly*) All right—it's true.

SEVIGNE Thank you. (*He seems content, goes on in a kindly tone*) You may smoke now, if you like.

JOSEFA You're being nice to me suddenly.

SEVIGNE We're nearly finished. We have the motive now.

JOSEFA (*Startled*) The—*what?*

SEVIGNE Your motive for the crime. Josefa Lantenay, I charge you with the murder of Miguel Ostos.

27

JOSEFA   Good for you! Say, is this a full-time job you have here?

SEVIGNE   You were found on the scene of the crime, with the murder weapon in your hand. Only the motive was missing.

JOSEFA   As long as it's my motive, is it all right to tell me what it was?

SEVIGNE   The lover who supplanted Ostos. That was your motive. To protect him from Ostos' jealous rage. (*To* MORESTAN) Have you got that?

MORESTAN   Every word.

JOSEFA   (*Plaintively, to* MORESTAN)   *You* look like a sensible fellow—you tell him this is silly—

SEVIGNE   Pay attention to me! Stand up.

JOSEFA   Now, don't you dare lay a finger on me!

SEVIGNE   *Stand up!* (*She stands*) We are now going to reconstruct the crime exactly as it happened.

JOSEFA   I told you how it happened. (*And then, resigned*) I knew this was coming . . . men!
   (*She starts to tug down the zipper of her dress*)

SEVIGNE   (*Outraged*)   Stop!

JOSEFA   (*Hand on zipper*)   Oh? You *don't* want it exactly as it happened? (*To* MORESTAN) Didn't he say "exactly"?

MORESTAN   (*Intrigued*)   As a matter of fact, he did.

SEVIGNE   Sit down! (*She shrugs, fixes her zipper, sits down*) What are the dimensions of your room?

JOSEFA It's a maid's room—don't you know what they are like? . . . No, chances are *you* wouldn't. (*At his impatience, exasperated*) I never measured it. I suppose it's about twelve feet long, eight or ten feet wide.

SEVIGNE How it is furnished?

JOSEFA A chest of drawers, small table, an armchair, a straight chair by the window . . . oh, yes, and a bed.

SEVIGNE How big a bed?

JOSEFA (*Coolly*) Big enough.

SEVIGNE You told Ostos that it was all over—that you had a new lover.

JOSEFA Yes, I had to do it. It seemed the decent thing to do. But I told him it was nothing, a passing fancy, just a little bit of foolishness—

SEVIGNE He didn't believe you, did he?

JOSEFA At first he did because I swore by the head of my papa —(*Adding wistfully*) Poor Papa! But then he started raving again. He swore he would find the man and kill him. He rushed to get his coat, still cursing and raving.

SEVIGNE What did you do?

JOSEFA Well, I couldn't chase him—I was barefoot. I told him to stop acting like an idiot and come to bed. (*Ruefully*) It was my own fault for trying to part friends.

SEVIGNE You didn't struggle with him for the gun?

JOSEFA What gun? We were in my bedroom, not a shooting gallery.

29

SEVIGNE Now, be sensible and listen to me. If you struggled with him, to get the gun away from him, it could have gone off by accident. An unpremeditated shooting. Under the circumstances, hardly a crime at all.

JOSEFA You've got this thing about guns . . .

SEVIGNE You said a moment ago that he was rushing out to find the man and kill him.

JOSEFA With a knife! (*Pityingly*) Really, you know very little about Spaniards.

SEVIGNE Not all of us have had your opportunities for research. However, what about Ostos' speech to the cook: he swore he'd find the man, and then—boom! boom!—it would be all over. Does that sound like a knife?

JOSEFA (*Trying it*) Boom! Boom! (*Candidly*) No, it doesn't. (*And again*) Boom! Boom! (*Gives up*) You've got me there. (SEVIGNE *is circling the chair, stalking her.* JOSEFA's *head turns with him, watching him warily*)

SEVIGNE (*Suddenly*) Did you know that a gun was kept in the glove compartment of the Rolls-Royce?

JOSEFA Which Rolls-Royce?

SEVIGNE What?

JOSEFA We have three.

SEVIGNE (*Startled*) You *have*? (*Fumbles in the file*) Let me see—ah, the limousine. (*Confronting her again*) Do you deny it?

JOSEFA How should I know what goes on in the limousine, or in the glove compartment? But in my bedroom, no guns.

SEVIGNE Very nice. What about the gun that was found in your hand?

JOSEFA *I* was unconscious.

SEVIGNE Conveniently. (*Takes a photo enlargement from the file*) Do you know what this is? It was made by experts in the police department. This—on the left—is a microscopic enlargement of a bullet fired from the pistol you had in your hand; this on the right is a similar study of the bullet taken from the body of Miguel Ostos.

JOSEFA Oh! How awful!

SEVIGNE They are identical!

JOSEFA What a disgusting thing to carry about with you!

SEVIGNE Furthermore, you had in your hand a thirty-eight caliber Biretta automatic pistol which has been identified as the gun kept in the Rolls-Royce. (*Adding quickly*) And don't say *which* Rolls-Royce! Ostos took it from the car, brought it to your room, and when he threatened—as you yourself have testified—that he would kill your lover, *you shot him!*

JOSEFA No! That's not true! I swear it!

SEVIGNE By the head of your papa? Poor Papa!

JOSEFA (*Wounded*) Oh! How can you hurt me so?

SEVIGNE You're lying and concealing information. That means I have to dig deeper. Don't blame me if I strike a nerve. Morestan—chalk!

    (MORESTAN *hands him chalk from the desk drawer*)

SEVIGNE (*To* JOSEFA) Get up! (*She rises*) Over there—(*Pointing to* MORESTAN'S *desk. She moves obediently.* SEVIGNE *kneels*) Now, then—(*He draws a rough rectangle on the floor*)—this is the shape of your room—

JOSEFA (*To* MORESTAN) Is he always like this?

SEVIGNE Pay attention! (*Indicating the chalk outline*) Show me the location of your bed. (*She hesitates*) Now, don't be coy. It seems to have been a landmark as well-known as the Eiffel Tower.

JOSEFA (*Outraged, she stamps her foot on the outline*) There! (SEVIGNE *makes an X on the spot*)

SEVIGNE The chest of drawers? (*Sullenly* JOSEFA *indicates the upper left of the outline, and* SEVIGNE *marks it with a small square. As he works*) The window—here, on the street side —right? (*He marks it*) The armchair, here, by the window —right? Now—the door? (JOSEFA *sullenly indicates it, and* SEVIGNE *marks it. He straightens up, tossing the chalk back to* MORESTAN. SEVIGNE, *confidently*) Now, then—the pure science of criminology will bring us to the truth . . . (*He peers at his drawing but having made it he isn't quite certain what to do with it*) Er—just study that. Fix it in your memory.

(*He turns to the desk for a quick flash at the books*)

JOSEFA I like it. In the house they have funny pictures like that—*millions* some of them cost—and not a bit better than yours. (*At his cold look—defensively*) You told me to study it!

SEVIGNE Now . . . think—were the lights in your room on, or off?

JOSEFA (*Flatly*) Off.

SEVIGNE You're positive?

JOSEFA Positive. With Miguel, it was always in the dark. (*Confidingly*) Poor Miguel! You see, he couldn't get over thinking it was a sin. Maybe it is, but turning out the lights doesn't change *that* and—the times I've stubbed my toe in the dark—

SEVIGNE You're wandering again. No reminiscing, *please!*

JOSEFA But these are memories of love! They're important!

SEVIGNE Another time. Now, just stick to the facts.

JOSEFA Why don't you listen—it might take your mind off guns and those dirty pictures of bullets—(*At his mounting impatience*) All right, the facts. There we were. The door opened, a shot was fired, he fell, and I fainted. (*At* SEVIGNE's *steady stare*) Well, you asked me. That's what you wanted—facts.

SEVIGNE Sit down. (*She sits*) Who else had a key to your room?

JOSEFA Nobody.

SEVIGNE Then how did the door open behind Ostos just before he was killed?

JOSEFA I don't know.

SEVIGNE This happened in the home of the banker Benjamin Beaurevers. Now, honestly, can you picture unknown intruders prowling in the halls, opening locked doors, firing shots, vanishing like ghosts . . . that's a ridiculous story.

JOSEFA (*Angrily*) Sure, it's ridiculous. It's the truth, that's why. Do you think *I* like it? When I told it to Inspector Colas he took my temperature; he thought I had fever. I wish I could tell a smooth, elegant story, but I'm telling you

33

what really happened. I know it's terrible and clumsy, but it's the truth, and it's all I have.

SEVIGNE Morestan, note that I am unimpressed by this outburst. Sit down. (*She sits*) What other visitors did you have?

JOSEFA (*Still sulking*) When?

SEVIGNE (*Patiently*) The night Ostos was killed.

JOSEFA I'm not allowed to have visitors in my room—(*Then sheepishly*) That *does* sound funny, I admit. But poor Miguel, I mean, he wasn't really a visitor.

SEVIGNE Please answer the question.

JOSEFA Oh, I thought I did.
  (*Her response is nervous*)

SEVIGNE Just a simple "yes" or "no" will do it.

JOSEFA It's simple for you, but my head is spinning with questions . . . and answers . . . I don't even know which is which.

SEVIGNE Is this really so difficult? On the night of the crime, other than Miguel Ostos, did you have any visitors in your room?

JOSEFA (*Cornered*) No!

SEVIGNE Thank you. So it narrows down to just you and the victim in your bedroom, doesn't it?

JOSEFA It's a small room.

SEVIGNE After the shot, you immediately fainted?

JOSEFA Right away. (*With a snap*) Like that!

SEVIGNE You fell beside the bed?

JOSEFA Yes. I can prove it because I've still got the bump from when I hit the bedpost on the way down.

SEVIGNE Indicate the exact spot, please . . . on the diagram. (*She points to it. He marks the spot*) Now, where was Ostos when the shot was fired?

JOSEFA There.
　　　　(*She indicates the place and he marks it*)

SEVIGNE (*Annoyed*) Very well. You and Ostos were about ten feet apart. . . . Is that right?

JOSEFA Yes . . . I suppose so.

SEVIGNE According to the police laboratory, the shot was fired from a distance of just about ten feet.

JOSEFA Of course. I told you all along: the shot was fired from the hall, when the door opened.

SEVIGNE Or from here—(*Indicating* JOSEFA'S *place in the diagram*)—from the bed—exactly ten feet away—*by you.*

JOSEFA Please! (*Then reasonably, pleading with him*) I am in my bedroom. I have nothing on—not a stitch—what would I be doing with a gun? *Where* would it be?

SEVIGNE Anywhere. Under the pillows . . . in the bedclothes . . .

JOSEFA You have a funny idea of what goes on in a girl's bedroom.

SEVIGNE Perhaps. I daresay it came as a surprise to Ostos, too. (*Then, with a touch of formality*) Are you acquainted with a lawyer who might represent you?

JOSEFA No.

SEVIGNE You'll need one.

JOSEFA　No. I don't want a lawyer. (*Glaring at him*) I know enough lawyers.

SEVIGNE　Knowing one more won't corrupt you. I'll see that counsel is assigned to your case.

JOSEFA　I tell you, I don't want a lawyer.

SEVIGNE　Don't be stubborn about this. Do you realize the trouble you're in?

JOSEFA　I'm choking on it.

SEVIGNE　There's more. Now, listen carefully. . . . Ostos didn't die at once. He lived for a few moments, and he talked.

JOSEFA　What? (*The cry is not for her own peril*) Oh, no! My poor Miguel! He saw himself dying? (*She covers her face with her hands*) Oh, why did you tell me?

SEVIGNE　Because he *talked*. Do you realize what that means? In the presence of witnesses, he said: "Josefa, why did you do it?"

JOSEFA　(*Shocked*)　He died that way . . . thinking I had killed him? Oh, Miguel, wherever you are now, you know I didn't do it.

SEVIGNE　It is a powerful accusation against you.

JOSEFA　I know. Poor Miguel—

SEVIGNE　Stop saying: "Poor Miguel!" His worries are over. Yours are just starting. (*Takes a paper from his desk*) Do you know what this is? A warrant for your arrest. The guard is waiting outside there to take you to prison. The next step is trial, then prison again—*or worse*.

JOSEFA (*An outburst*)   Why? Do I look like a killer, or sound like one? Miguel and I were lovers once, and he was still dear to me. *Why* would I kill him?

SEVIGNE   I told you why. To protect someone. The man you love now.

JOSEFA   I swear that's not true!

SEVIGNE (*Attacking*)   Then give me his name! (*She stiffens at once*) Come on—out with it—quickly—the name of the man!

JOSEFA   If the warrant is ready, I'm ready.
(SEVIGNE *studies her, she drops her gaze*)

SEVIGNE   Suddenly, you're hard, and determined.

JOSEFA   Can't I just go to prison, without speeches?

SEVIGNE   You won't give me the name of the man?

JOSEFA   No!

SEVIGNE   And you say you couldn't have killed Ostos to protect this man? When right here and now you're risking everything for him?

JOSEFA   That's my affair.

SEVIGNE   Mine, too. Because it proves what you're capable of.

JOSEFA   You know very little about justice—and nothing about love.

SEVIGNE   Well, perhaps I'll learn from you—as Ostos did.

JOSEFA   Oh! (*She flings the handkerchief at him*) You're heartless!
(SEVIGNE *opens the door, beckons to the* GUARD *who enters.* SEVIGNE *hands him the warrant*)

SEVIGNE Take her away! (*The* GUARD *puts his hand on her arm; she shakes it off angrily. She turns to look at* SEVIGNE *again.* SEVIGNE, *irritably*) Oh, get her out of here!
(*He avoids looking at her*)

JOSEFA (*Quietly, to the* GUARD) I'm ready.
(*The* GUARD *leads her out; the door closes.* SEVIGNE *sinks wearily into the witness's chair*)

MORESTAN Very good. Extremely well handled. The fact is, I thought you were about to get your confession, and if you had pressed that final accusation a bit harder—

SEVIGNE Don't be an ass!

MORESTAN (*Startled*) What?

SEVIGNE She's innocent.

MORESTAN (*Floundering*) Innocent? Surely not—the evidence —the file—the way you questioned her—

SEVIGNE I hammered her to show her the danger she was in. If she talks long enough—the idiot!—she'll chatter herself right up the steps to the guillotine.

MORESTAN Innocent! (*Shrugs helplessly*) Maybe, but where does that leave *us*?

SEVIGNE (*Angrily*) It leaves us with a nice, juicy, *un*solved murder.

MORESTAN (*Pained*) The Chief Prosecutor *hates* those! You're quite sure she's innocent? What I mean to say is, if we have to give somebody the benefit of the doubt, let's give it to the Chief Prosecutor.

SEVIGNE   Come on, let's lock up. For my first day, I've had about enough.

(*He starts to gather up the precious lawbooks on his desk, looking at the bulky volume in his hand*)

MORESTAN   A magistrate—reading lawbooks all day! I knew this would happen!

Curtain

ACT TWO

The scene is the same as Act One.

It is a bright, sunny winter afternoon, two days later. MORESTAN *is alone in the chamber, hard at work transcribing various documents and bits of testimony. He works with an air of disapproval. The door opens slowly, rather timidly, and in the same fashion* ANTOINETTE SEVIGNE *enters.*

ANTOINETTE   Hello . . . am I disturbing you?

MORESTAN   No . . . not a bit. Come on in. (*She is looking around for the missing member*) He won't be long. He's with the Chief Prosecutor.

ANTOINETTE (*Apprehensively*)   The Chief Prosecutor? Was—it because of the newspapers?

MORESTAN   Probably.

ANTOINETTE   But it wasn't Paul's fault. He was only doing his duty!

MORESTAN   No more, no less. Your husband is absolutely fair and fearless, passionately concerned with the administration of justice. Those are wonderful qualities! (*With a sigh*) If only he weren't a magistrate!

ANTOINETTE   Is the Chief difficult?

MORESTAN   When the Chief was on the bench, he was known as Judge Necessity—Judge Necessity—get it? Because necessity knows no law!

ANTOINETTE (*Dutifully*)   Oh! Oh! that's a good one.
          (*A hollow tinkle of laughter*)

43

MORESTAN Excuse me. I'll go on with my work. We take up the investigation in a little while.

ANTOINETTE Yes, I know. Go right ahead.

(MORESTAN *resumes his copying or transcribing.* ANTOINETTE *fidgets around the office a bit, picking up a text or magazine, putting it down again.* MORESTAN, *meanwhile, looks up from his work to get paper, and* ANTOINETTE, *of course, takes the opportunity to pick up the conversation*)

ANTOINETTE (*Quite artlessly*) What is she like?

MORESTAN She? Oh—*she.*
(*He shrugs, baffled*)

ANTOINETTE Is she pretty?

MORESTAN Yes . . .

ANTOINETTE The photograph in the paper this morning didn't look very pretty.

MORESTAN She is. Not at first sight, but later one is aware of it.

ANTOINETTE Do *you* think she's innocent?

MORESTAN She says she is.

ANTOINETTE But don't they all say that?

MORESTAN She says it differently.

ANTOINETTE It's not fair! We've just arrived, we haven't even found an apartment. Why couldn't Paul get something nice, a white-collar case like a bank robbery—why should he have *this*? (*Furiously*) And what right has she got to be innocent?

MORESTAN (*Vaguely*) Who knows? . . . The criminal mind . . .

44

ANTOINETTE And Paul is always for the underdog. It's a compulsion. Even if there isn't any underdog, he finds a dog and *puts* him under.

(*She subsides, glancing at some ancient magazines, and in a moment* SEVIGNE *enters. He doesn't instantly see his wife*)

SEVIGNE Ah, Morestan, you should have heard the old boy. Really remarkable lung power for a man of his years—(*And then*) Antoinette! What a nice surprise!

ANTOINETTE What happened, Paul?

SEVIGNE Well . . . the Chief began with a ringing affirmation of the great guiding principle of the courts: equal justice under law. And then he closed by swearing he'd kick my ass all the way back to Lyons.

ANTOINETTE Paul!

SEVIGNE He was joking, of course. (*Without conviction*) The Chief has a fantastic sense of humor, hasn't he, Morestan?

MORESTAN Fantastic.

ANTOINETTE It's inconvenient, isn't it, that you think the girl is innocent?

SEVIGNE Yes, very—for any number of people apparently. One funny chattering idiot of a girl, and so much money and influence pushing her into a quiet, cozy little cell. (*Wistfully*) Did you know that Benjamin Beaurevers has three Rolls-Royces? I have one Simca, vintage 1953, and Josefa Lantenay has only a second-hand bicycle. On sheer horsepower we are definitely outclassed.

ANTOINETTE (*Outraged*) *We?* That's *us*—you and I!

45

SEVIGNE I'm not forgetting that.

MORESTAN (*Embarrassed*) Er—perhaps I ought to see about the—er—witness—

SEVIGNE Sit down, Morestan. (*To* ANTOINETTE) What do you think I should do?

ANTOINETTE (*Confused, angry*) I don't know. But if your superiors want something done a certain way, then it's their responsibility, isn't it?

SEVIGNE Up to a point, yes.

ANTOINETTE Then do it! It's nothing but sheer ego to defy them. You're jeopardizing your career and everything we've worked for.

SEVIGNE Antoinette, I assure you—on my honor and my experience—that I believe the girl is innocent.

ANTOINETTE Innocent! A little tramp who doesn't even wear underpants!

SEVIGNE If she were charged with that I wouldn't lift a finger to help her, but she's accused of murder. I have to care about that. Not about her—*it*. Justice.

ANTOINETTE That's pompous and pretentious.

SEVIGNE Is it? (*Thoughtfully*) Yes, I suppose it is. It shouldn't be. I'm a lawyer . . . and a magistrate . . . surely I ought to be able to say the word justice without sounding like a stuffed shirt.

ANTOINETTE Oh, Paul, you're such a schoolboy. You can be hoodwinked into anything.

SEVIGNE You ought to know.
  (*He takes her in his arms*)

46

ANTOINETTE   Will you stop this nonsense about the girl?

SEVIGNE   It's too late, I'm afraid. I'm sorry. I tried to warn you. Remember? Even before we were married, I told you I was a man of integrity—and you seemed pleased.

ANTOINETTE   (*Ruefully*)   I thought you were lying. A lawyer— I never dreamed you were telling the truth.

SEVIGNE   We're tricky. (*Kisses her lightly*) Now, run along.

ANTOINETTE   All right. (*He has already turned to his table*) Are you going to question the girl again?

SEVIGNE   We'll start with her.
   (ANTOINETTE *has picked up her purse and her gloves; she drops the gloves on the desk again*)

ANTOINETTE   (*Sweetly*)   Goodbye, darling. Get home as soon as you can.

SEVIGNE   I promise.

ANTOINETTE   Goodbye, Monsieur Morestan.

MORESTAN   Goodbye, Madame Sevigne.

SEVIGNE   (*As she is nearly out*)   Antoinette . . . (*She turns*) Take your gloves.
   (*He rises, hands them to her.* ANTOINETTE *smiles, but she is annoyed*)

ANTOINETTE   Thank you, darling. It was silly of me to leave them.

SEVIGNE   No, not a bit silly. You wanted an excuse to come back for a look at Josefa Lantenay. (*Giving her a little pat*) Run along, now.

47

ANTOINETTE Really!

> (*She sweeps out with as much dignity as she can manage under the circumstances.* SEVIGNE *gets back to his desk and the papers*)

SEVIGNE Morestan, when I'm questioning the girl, I shall ask you to bring in another witness—for confrontation.

MORESTAN Yes—who?

SEVIGNE No matter. But when I do, take your time.

MORESTAN Eh?

SEVIGNE Fiddle with papers, tie a shoelace—anything, but *take your time*.

MORESTAN (*Plaintively*) Indefinitely?

SEVIGNE A few moments . . . you'll be able to judge for your-self. (*Glancing at his watch*) See if she's here. Bring her in.

> (MORESTAN *goes to the door, beckons.* JOSEFA *enters. She is pale, wears no makeup; her hair is disheveled; she looks ravishing. She seems very subdued, glances at* SEVIGNE *on her entrance, then avoids his eyes*)

SEVIGNE Sit down, Mademoiselle.

> (JOSEFA *shuffles to the indicated chair, is about to sit*)

JOSEFA Mademoiselle! (*She looks at* SEVIGNE *suspiciously*) You called me Mademoiselle. One of your tricks?

SEVIGNE Sit down, Mademoiselle.

JOSEFA (*Seated*) I don't think anyone ever called me that. It's always, "Hey, you!" or just, "Hurry Josefa!" or, "Be careful with that broom, stupid!"—but never Mademoiselle. To get that, I had to go to prison first. (*Grudgingly, to* SEVIGNE) But, thanks, anyway.

SEVIGNE You're welcome. Now, then, to resume, I would like to—

JOSEFA Oh, that prison! (*Accusingly*) Do you know what it's like?

SEVIGNE (*Patiently*) If you'll just listen—

JOSEFA How would you like it if two dirty old women stripped *you* to the skin, and searched you—everywhere— horribly?

SEVIGNE Prison is supposed to be unpleasant. (*Pointedly*) So people will try to avoid being put in it. Now, will you please listen—

JOSEFA And this picture they took of me! (*She fishes a newspaper clipping from her pocket*) Look at that—I look terrible!

SEVIGNE How did you get that. Prisoners aren't allowed newspapers.

JOSEFA Ha! A lot you know. In a women's prison, the first few days, you can get anything. The other girls buzz around you, offering you extra food, candy, newspapers . . . oh, you pay, don't worry, and tonight or tomorrow night they'll be coming around to me . . . (*With a gesture of disgust*) Your prison!

SEVIGNE It is not my prison. And stop babbling.

JOSEFA All right. I'll be good. Just don't put me back in that horrible hole. I'll do anything. I'll confess, if you'll let me go.

SEVIGNE Shut up . . . and *listen!*

JOSEFA Yes, sir. (*She winces as she sees him take the file. As he turns back to her*) What do you want me to tell you?

49

SEVIGNE We have some unfinished business, you and I. Now, then: the name of your lover?

JOSEFA (*Promptly*) Miguel Ostos. (*And at* SEVIGNE's *stern look, plaintively*) Well, he *was*—

SEVIGNE The other man.

JOSEFA He left town weeks ago . . . and, really, he's got nothing to do with all this . . .

SEVIGNE I'm not surprised that Ostos beat you.

JOSEFA I know. Even Miguel said he did it only in self-defense, when I was being too much of an idiot.

SEVIGNE Do you want to go back to prison?

JOSEFA (*Meekly*) No—I'd rather you beat me.

SEVIGNE I'll ask you just once more, and I warn you—
    (*He stops short as the door opens and* ANTOINETTE *enters*)

ANTOINETTE (*Brazenly*) Oh, darling, forgive me—I forgot my gloves.

SEVIGNE *What?*
    (MORESTAN *leans way over his writing to conceal his amusement*)

ANTOINETTE I must have left them on a chair, or on your desk . . .
    (*Looks for them, but with her eyes plainly riveted on* JOSEFA. JOSEFA, *embarrassed, pulls her skirt down as far as it will go, apparently the only gesture of modesty she knows*)

William Shatner, Julie Harris, and Diana van der Vlis, as SEVIGNE, JOSEFA, and ANTOINETTE SEVIGNE

SEVIGNE Antoinette! Will you kindly leave us—(*Sternly*)—at once!

ANTOINETTE Ah, here they are!
(*Pretending to take them from under a book on the desk*)

SEVIGNE (*Seething*) All right—now go! (ANTOINETTE *is pulling the gloves on, finger by finger, studying* JOSEFA) Antoinette!

ANTOINETTE Yes, darling. Just going. (*Ominously*) Get home as early as you can—we have a lot to talk about.
(*She goes, slamming the door*)

JOSEFA (*Curiously*) Your wife? (SEVIGNE, *still seething, ignores her, getting himself in hand again for the interrogation*) You married a young one, eh? (*In a tone of respect*) It's funny . . . I didn't think you were the type.

SEVIGNE Are there any other comments you want to make about my wife?

JOSEFA (*Unenthusiastically*) She's very pretty.

SEVIGNE Thanks. (*Dryly*) She liked you, too. Now then—the name of the man? (*As she stares back at him*) Ah, you're being your sweet, reasonable self again, eh?

JOSEFA I want to be. I cried for eleven hours in that filthy cell. The other women said it was a new record for the prison. And if you send me back, it will be worse . . .

SEVIGNE So?

JOSEFA I *won't* give you the name of someone innocent, and let you get him mixed up in this. . . . I call that being an informer.

SEVIGNE I guarantee you that in a few minutes you'll give me the name.

JOSEFA All right. I don't mind waiting—(*And at the look in his eye*) That's right. Go on—hit me!

SEVIGNE How did you get on with your employer?

JOSEFA (*Enthusiastically*) Madame Beaurevers. She's marvelous. We're all crazy about her. She's been more like a wonderful older sister than an employer to me.

SEVIGNE When Inspector Colas asked you about Madame, you said . . . (*From the file*) "She's all right—if you like the snooty, icebox type."

JOSEFA *I* said that? About Madame? (*Conscience-stricken, emphatically*) I'm an ungrateful pig.

SEVIGNE And Monsieur Beaurevers?

JOSEFA Well . . . He's very elegant, you know. (*With a hint of care*) He's probably very nice, too, but quite honestly, I never really understood most of what he was saying.

SEVIGNE Did you have many conversations?

JOSEFA Well, as a parlormaid, in *his* parlor, naturally, he had to tell me things. Don't you talk to *your* parlormaid?

SEVIGNE I will, when I have one. So you didn't get along with Monsieur Beaurevers?

JOSEFA Well, I wouldn't say that. But you see what I am—a simple girl, and I talk too much—and Monsieur Beaurevers is a banker, from a noble family, really terrifically well-bred.

SEVIGNE In other words, there was a gulf between you?

JOSEFA That's right—a real gulf.

SEVIGNE   Were you and Ostos on vacation together?

JOSEFA   No. Miguel went to the Basque country because there were great bullfights in Dax, Bayonne, Biarritz—all over. Dominguín and Ordóñez! Mano a mano! He couldn't miss those! (*Sadly*) Poor Miguel!

SEVIGNE   And you?

JOSEFA   Oh, I stayed with the family, at their country house. So near home for me. I could be with my old papa.

SEVIGNE   In October, you were all back in Paris. And Ostos' day off was changed?

JOSEFA   (*Innocently*)   Oh? Was that when that happened?

SEVIGNE   Yes. And Miguel Ostos began raving about his jealousy.

JOSEFA   (*Carefully*)   You ought to remember he was always raving about *something*. If it wasn't me, it was the Paris weather, or French food, or cowardly bulls—he never just talked, he raved.

SEVIGNE   (*From the file*)   Police interrogation of the cook: "A week after we came back to Paris, in October, Miguel said that Josefa had turned against him. 'I was a fool to let her go to the country alone,' he cried. 'She's been tripping over roots again down there, and without *me*.'"
   (*He glances at* JOSEFA *for comment*)

JOSEFA   That cook—still giving me heartburn!

SEVIGNE   What happened at Hauterive in September?

JOSEFA   (*Carefully*)   Well, it rained part of the time . . . I saw quite a lot of Papa . . . (*Glances up at him to see how she's*

53

doing) . . . had picnics and went swimming with some of the boys and girls I knew from the old days . . . that sort of thing, nothing much.

SEVIGNE   Did you enjoy your holiday?

JOSEFA   M-m-m-m . . . It was nice. Dull, but nice. (*She looks up at him, searching for some clue to this line of questioning. He is blank*) Why are you so interested in my vacation?

SEVIGNE   I'm not, really. Just passing the time. (*Casually*) Morestan, show in the witness Benjamin Beaurevers.
   (JOSEFA *comes straight up in her chair excitedly.* MORES-TAN, *following orders, putters about on his desk*)

JOSEFA   Monsieur Beaurevers—he is *here?*

SEVIGNE   (*Ignoring her*)   Hurry, Morestan!

MORESTAN   I'm hurrying.

JOSEFA   The way I look! They took everything away from me in prison—powder, lipstick, *everything.* (*She bites her lips to give them color, smooths her hair, looks in the window in lieu of a mirror, fixing herself up as best she can*) Oh, why does he have to see me looking like this? (MORESTAN *has gone to the door,* SEVIGNE *is looking at* JOSEFA *gravely, and she is suddenly aware of what she has betrayed*) Oh!
   (*She turns from the window slowly, facing him*)

SEVIGNE   Remember—I said you would give me the name of the man?

JOSEFA   (*Coldly*)   Are you happy doing this kind of work, Monsieur?

SEVIGNE   Try not to hate me too much.

54

JOSEFA I've never hated anyone. And I don't hate you. But don't be surprised if you hate yourself.

SEVIGNE (*Roughly*) Idiot! Must you be tricked into helping yourself?

JOSEFA Idiot? Because I won't betray someone? Thank you!

SEVIGNE All right, Joan of Arc—sit down.
(*At the door,* MADAME BEAUREVERS *is pushing past* MORESTAN, *who is trying to keep her out*)

MORESTAN Your interrogation is *later,* Madame.

MADAME BEAUREVERS Not at all. You've misunderstood.
(*She is very beautiful, chic, and carries the situation with an air of great gaiety*)

MORESTAN No, Madame, there is no mistake. Please wait.
(BENJAMIN BEAUREVERS *has followed his wife into the chamber. He is supremely elegant, quite handsome, very sure of himself. He makes no effort whatever to conform to any surroundings that are foreign to him.* MADAME BEAUREVERS *is instantly intent on charming* SEVIGNE)

MADAME BEAUREVERS (*Extending her hand*) My dear Judge, I was just explaining to your clerk—

SEVIGNE I'm not a judge, Madame—only a magistrate. Will you be kind enough—

MADAME BEAUREVERS (*Interrupting him*) Charming! What a cozy little office you have here! (*Glancing around the shabby interior*) Strange, isn't it—I feel quite at home here. Perhaps because so many friends and relatives are in the judiciary.

SEVIGNE Thank you, Madame. If you will be kind enough to wait in the corridor ...

MADAME BEAUREVERS (*One word at a time*) Wait? In—the—corridor?

SEVIGNE Or, if you prefer, in this adjoining room.
(*He indicates the door at left*)

MADAME BEAUREVERS But surely, you wouldn't think of questioning my husband alone—without me?

SEVIGNE In my opinion, Madame, that would be best.

MADAME BEAUREVERS Ridiculous! Why can't I be present?

SEVIGNE Because in this office, Madame, it is I who give orders, and with all due respect, I must ask you to wait outside.

MADAME BEAUREVERS (*Ominously*) Benjamin, did you hear that?

BEAUREVERS I did, my dear Dominique.

MADAME BEAUREVERS Is that all you have to say?

BEAUREVERS No doubt our learned friend could have expressed himself with more affability, but he may perhaps be pressed for time.

JOSEFA (*Aside, to* SEVIGNE) Fantastic, isn't it? I never understand half of what he says.

MADAME BEAUREVERS (*Turning to* JOSEFA) And we have you to thank, Josefa, for all this unpleasantness.

JOSEFA (*Indifferently*) So it seems, Madame.

MADAME BEAUREVERS And to think I have always had such confidence in you! And I was kind to you!

JOSEFA Very kind, Madame.

56

SEVIGNE Morestan, please show Madame Beaurevers to the corridor—at once.

MADAME BEAUREVERS (*Ominously*) Benjamin!

BEAUREVERS Yes, my dear Dominique?

MADAME BEAUREVERS Do you hear the tone of voice in which this man speaks to me?

BEAUREVERS I detected no coarseness or undue lack of courtesy in his address, my dear.

MADAME BEAUREVERS (*Furiously*) Very well, I'll wait.

SEVIGNE Thank you, Madame.
(MADAME BEAUREVERS *exits, slamming the door.* MORESTAN *returns to his place*)

BEAUREVERS I must explain to you, my dear Judge, that Dominique—Madame Beaurevers—does not mean to be overbearing, but hers is an ancient family, descended, I believe, in a direct line from Attila the Hun.

SEVIGNE Please sit down.

BEAUREVERS Thank you, my dear Judge.

SEVIGNE I am not a judge—only a magistrate. (*Glances at* MORESTAN *to see if he is ready, then to* BEAUREVERS) Your full name, please, address and profession.

BEAUREVERS Benjamin Beaurevers, one twelve rue de la Faisanderie, banker.

JOSEFA (*Solicitously*) You've lost weight, Monsieur.

BEAUREVERS A little. And you don't look too well, my poor Josefa.

JOSEFA Oh, well, the prison—you know—they don't let us have makeup.

BEAUREVERS Prison! Poor Josefa!

JOSEFA Oh, don't worry about me. You know I can look after myself—

> (SEVIGNE *has been tapping, louder and louder, with a pencil. It finally communicates itself to both* BEAUREVERS *and* JOSEFA, *who look at him*)

SEVIGNE (*Apologetically*) Thank you. It's rude of me to interrupt, but we have this murder on our hands. . . .

BEAUREVERS (*Heartily*) Of course. (*And to* JOSEFA) Pay attention, Josefa.

JOSEFA Yes, sir. (*Then sotto voce, indicating* SEVIGNE) Don't worry—he's nice. (*Waggles her finger chummily at* SEVIGNE, *who is stupefied by this intimacy. She goes on whispering to* BEAUREVERS) At first I didn't think so, and he *did* send me to prison, but he's really very nice.

SEVIGNE Be quiet!

JOSEFA (*Amiably*) Yes, sir.

SEVIGNE (*To* BEAUREVERS) Now, then, after you had returned to Paris in October, why was Ostos' day off changed from Wednesday to Thursday?

BEAUREVERS (*Carelessly*) I suppose it was due to some idiosyncrasy of household management.

SEVIGNE Would you mind using simpler language in your replies?

BEAUREVERS I wouldn't mind, but I don't know how.

SEVIGNE Did you personally order the change?

BEAUREVERS No. (*Adding*) Is that simple enough?

SEVIGNE Did you know that Miguel Ostos had been the lover of Josefa Lantenay?

BEAUREVERS I share the philosophy of the late Emperor Frederick the Great: "In my State," declared His Majesty, "every man shall amuse himself as he sees fit."

SEVIGNE Furthermore, that in addition to Ostos, there was another man?

BEAUREVERS Ah, youth, youth!

SEVIGNE Did you know the identity of the other man?

BEAUREVERS Without infringing on the rights and privileges of your high office, may *I* ask a question?

SEVIGNE Please . . .

BEAUREVERS Do *you* know the identity of the other man?

SEVIGNE I think so . . . yes.

BEAUREVERS Ah! . . . (*Then, carefully*) I feel a natural apprehension about my wife, you understand . . . do you suppose we can continue to share the secret between us?

SEVIGNE I hope so.

JOSEFA I swear I told him nothing. But my idiot face betrayed me when you were announced.

SEVIGNE Then you admit that you are the man?

BEAUREVERS I do, and with pleasure.

JOSEFA Thank you for saying that. And simply, so I could understand it.

SEVIGNE (*To* BEAUREVERS)   Do you know how to shut her up?

BEAUREVERS   Frankly, not for very long—and that only by a method I should hesitate to employ before witnesses of either sex.

SEVIGNE   Where did your affair begin—and when?

BEAUREVERS   At our country house, in Hauterive, in September.

JOSEFA (*Promptly*)   Thursday, eleventh September, just after twelve noon.

BEAUREVERS   Yes, I remember that I was starting to think about lunch.

SEVIGNE (*Dryly*)   And something put it out of your mind?

BEAUREVERS   Man cannot live by bread alone.

SEVIGNE   It was sudden, was it?

BEAUREVERS   To say that I had been for some time becoming aware of Josefa would not be entirely untruthful.

SEVIGNE   Are you answering "yes" or "no"?

BEAUREVERS   I am answering—the rest is up to you.

SEVIGNE   All right. Now then, back to your country house, September eleventh, just before lunch. Will you kindly take it from there?

BEAUREVERS   The country, in September, is not quite the live-liest atmosphere in France, you understand. My wife has her horses, and friends who ride and hunt, but strange as it may seem to you, I am not the outdoor type.

SEVIGNE   I accept that.

BEAUREVERS The indoor life, in fact, often yields rather more adventure.

SEVIGNE I know. That's why we're all here.

JOSEFA (*To* BEAUREVERS) He doesn't like it when you keep on straying from the point.

BEAUREVERS Oh. My apologies. (*Groping for the main thread of the enquiry*) Er—where were we?

JOSEFA (*Gently prodding his memory*) The library at Hauterive . . . I was waxing the floor . . . remember?

BEAUREVERS (*Beaming*) Ah, yes. How could I forget? (*To* SEVIGNE) A superb room. Almost fifty feet in length and thirty across. Josefa is an excellent worker, you know, and she had the floor gleaming like a skating rink. Unfortunately— or fortunately—depending on the point of view—soon after I entered, she tripped—

SEVIGNE And fell?

BEAUREVERS (*Surprised*) Just so.

SEVIGNE You jumped forward to help her, and then you both fell?

BEAUREVERS But, my dear chap, that's precisely what happened! How did you know?

SEVIGNE Statistics. Continue.

BEAUREVERS (*Delicately*) Well, there we were, slipping and sliding—to be entirely truthful, I must tell you that she wears very little in the way of—

JOSEFA (*Cheerfully*) Oh, he knows that.

BEAUREVERS (*Taken aback*) Oh! (*Respectfully, to* SEVIGNE) I must say that your examinations are extremely thorough.

SEVIGNE And that is when Josefa Lantenay became your mistress?

BEAUREVERS (*Astounded*) My *what?*

JOSEFA (*Gently*) He means *me.*

BEAUREVERS (*Honestly surprised*) But of course! You *are* my mistress! (*Apologetically, to both*) I had never thought of it in precisely that way. (*To* SEVIGNE) Semantically, of course, you are entirely correct.

SEVIGNE Semantically, biologically, legally, that is the fact, isn't it?

BEAUREVERS (*Emphatically*) Oh, yes!

SEVIGNE And from then on? . . .

BEAUREVERS I had not intended to embark on a prolonged relationship—(*To* JOSEFA)—I mean no offense, my dear.

JOSEFA I didn't even know you were talking about me.

BEAUREVERS (*To* SEVIGNE) But—as I had already inferred— Hauterive in September offers only limited and monotonous amusements, and Josefa . . . (*A sigh of memory*) My learned friend, this girl is more attractive than you would think possible!

SEVIGNE And Ostos?

BEAUREVERS Not nearly as attractive. (*With a tolerant shrug*) Of course, if your taste runs to sullen Spanish chauffeurs . . .

SEVIGNE I meant, how did Ostos react?

JOSEFA   Miguel knew nothing.

BEAUREVERS   He was on vacation in the Basque country. An aficionado. He had the Spanish passion for bullfights.

JOSEFA (*Beaming*)   Ole! ... Ole!

BEAUREVERS (*Indulgently*)   Precisely. Ole! Ole!
(*They look at each other very fondly, lost to their surroundings.* SEVIGNE *draws them back by tapping sharply with his pencil*)

SEVIGNE   Now, when you returned to Paris in October, what about Ostos then?

BEAUREVERS   As you have surmised, my learned friend, it was found expedient to change his free day. On other occasions it was relatively simple to find or invent an errand for him in some remote part of the city. Even in the suburbs. Once when I was coming back from the South, he waited all night long at Orly Field for my plane. Actually, I arrived at dinner time—at Le Bourget—and came home quietly by taxi. (*Smiling at* JOSEFA) Remember?

JOSEFA   M-m-m-m-m! (*And then*) Miguel caught cold waiting and he cursed and sneezed for two days.

BEAUREVERS   It was marvelous being with Josefa, while he waited all night at the wrong airport.

JOSEFA (*Cautiously, to* SEVIGNE)   It was the idea of the joke, you understand—there was no real anger between Monsieur Beaurevers and Miguel—

BEAUREVERS   Nonsense—I detested him.

SEVIGNE   Before your affair with Josefa—or since?

BEAUREVERS Oh, long before. For one thing, he was well over six feet, and I usually take an instant dislike to anyone taller than I am. (*Amending it*) Naturally, that's not true of General De Gaulle.

SEVIGNE Your dislike of Ostos was based entirely on altitude?

BEAUREVERS No. It's true that he was a tall, handsome brute, and looked very well in uniform, but there was also a baffling air of insolence about him. He seemed to resent being ordered to do this or that.

JOSEFA That's true. It was his pride. He complained bitterly. "Just because I'm a chauffeur and a valet," he said, "they treat me like a servant."

SEVIGNE (*To* BEAUREVERS) Why did you keep him in your employ?

BEAUREVERS At first because he was a skilled chauffeur . . . and then, afterwards, I was afraid that if I sent him packing, he might take Josefa with him.

JOSEFA Ah, that was kind. Thank you.

BEAUREVERS Not at all. (*And to* SEVIGNE) In any event, the problem of Ostos no longer exists.

SEVIGNE Yes, that's certainly true, isn't it? Couldn't be better if you had arranged it yourself, could it?

BEAUREVERS (*Unruffled*) If you are speaking as a member of the staff of the Prosecutor, it would perhaps be best if I made no comment.

SEVIGNE Why was a gun kept in the glove compartment of the Rolls-Royce?

BEAUREVERS (*Innocently*) Which Rolls-Royce?

SEVIGNE (*Resigned*)   I let myself in for that, didn't I? All right, the limousine. *Don't* tell me it was standard equipment.

BEAUREVERS   The vehicle in question is actually owned by our bank. (*Delicately*) Some aspect of taxation is involved. It is sometimes used for inconspicuous transfers of large sums ... valuables.

SEVIGNE   In any event, you knew it was there?

BEAUREVERS   I *put* it there.

SEVIGNE   And you're familiar with ordinary firearms?

BEAUREVERS   My dear fellow, I was one of the best shots in France.

JOSEFA   He gave it up. He's too kind to kill anything. (*Helping all she can*) And he won't admit it, but now his eyesight is terrible.

SEVIGNE   If Monsieur Beaurevers wants a lawyer, why don't you let him choose one? (*And back to* BEAUREVERS) You were the first in the room after Ostos was shot?

BEAUREVERS   Yes ... that is so.

SEVIGNE   You hesitate?

BEAUREVERS   Only because I believe it is a question of some importance. (*Firmly*) I was the first.

SEVIGNE   You were attracted to the scene by the shot?

BEAUREVERS   Yes. I was in my dressing room. At first I thought it might have been the backfire from a car, but in our street, cars don't do that. So—I rushed downstairs to investigate.

SEVIGNE   On entering the room, what did you see?

BEAUREVERS   Josefa was lying at the foot of the bed . . .
(*He hesitates*)

SEVIGNE   Yes, go on.

BEAUREVERS   She was nude . . .

SEVIGNE   Yes, that fact has been established by *all* the witnesses.

BEAUREVERS   My immediate concern, of course, was for Josefa, but I saw at once that she was unharmed. Her chest was rising and falling regularly, in a manner both tranquil and profound . . . rising and falling . . .
(*His voice becomes quite bemused with the memory*)

SEVIGNE (*Dryly*)   You didn't also happen to notice the body of Miguel Ostos anywhere in the room?

BEAUREVERS (*Recalled*)   Oh, yes. (*Matter of fact*) He was lying just inside the door. I had to step over him, in fact, to get to Josefa. (*Adding*) Which I did.

SEVIGNE   Ostos was still alive, was he not?

BEAUREVERS   He was.

SEVIGNE   He was quite conscious?

BEAUREVERS   Well, he was alive . . . gasping . . .

SEVIGNE   He was trying to speak . . . to say something?

BEAUREVERS (*Reluctantly*)   I had that impression, yes.

SEVIGNE (*Patiently*)   Could you clearly understand what he was trying to say?

BEAUREVERS   Well, you know, a foreigner, under the best conditions his accent was quite coarse, not at all Parisian. Also, he was a type who spoke wildly at all times, even when he had not been shot.

SEVIGNE What were his exact words?

BEAUREVERS A dying man . . . and you quibble about exact words?

SEVIGNE *Approximately* what were his exact words?
(BEAUREVERS *looks pained, and* JOSEFA *leaps into the breach*)

JOSEFA It's unfair to ask Monsieur Beaurevers that question in front of me.

BEAUREVERS Thank you for understanding, Josefa. (*To* SEVIGNE) Sensitive! It's quite amazing, really. She's had little or no education.

SEVIGNE What did Ostos say? I must insist that you answer.

JOSEFA I'll answer. Miguel said: "Josefa, why did you do it?" He said it over and over again.

SEVIGNE Why do you answer? Did you hear the words spoken?

JOSEFA I was unconscious. I'm repeating what you told me.

SEVIGNE And I am repeating what Monsieur Beaurevers told the police. (*At* BEAUREVERS' *pained look*) That's true, isn't it?

BEAUREVERS (*Reluctantly*) Yes. Actually, it was my wife who mentioned it to Inspector Colas . . .

SEVIGNE But it was you who heard Ostos say it? It remains the principal cause of her incrimination.

JOSEFA Nonsense! What about the gun in my hand? (*Comfortingly, to* BEAUREVERS) Pay no attention, Monsieur Beaurevers—there is plenty of evidence against me.

BEAUREVERS I have the impression that you are reproaching me for aiding justice in this affair.

JOSEFA Very good. (*To* SEVIGNE) What do you say to that?

SEVIGNE (*To* BEAUREVERS) I was merely surprised that you could so blithely incriminate a girl who has meant something to you.

BEAUREVERS It was not something that I enjoyed doing, you understand—

SEVIGNE At any rate, your statement to the police incriminates her on the unverifiable words of a dead man.

BEAUREVERS I am not entirely sure that I like the implications of the word "unverifiable." Are you making the point that I invented these words?

SEVIGNE Well, it is possible that you might have invented them.

JOSEFA (*Indignant*) Oh! (*To* BEAUREVERS) Don't let him say such wicked things. Tell him who you are!

BEAUREVERS It takes so long.

SEVIGNE (*Sternly*) The point at issue is the statement allegedly made by a dying man. In a murder case, that is crucial.

BEAUREVERS Why? If I were dying, I might say anything.

SEVIGNE In a less sophisticated environment, the assumption is that in these circumstances one tells the truth. (*And then, angrily*) Damn it! You've got me talking that way!

BEAUREVERS I am honored.

SEVIGNE I'm not. Bluntly, then, you were the first person in the room after Ostos was shot. The girl is unconscious, Ostos is dying. You are alone. You have the opportunity to put into Ostos' mouth words that seem useful.

JOSEFA   That's the silliest thing I ever heard!

SEVIGNE   (*Ominously*)   Oh, is it?

JOSEFA   Yes, it is. Words like: "Josefa, why did you do it?" If Monsieur Beaurevers made up that sentence, it would be five times longer and nobody would know what it meant.

BEAUREVERS   A valid point. As you yourself have observed, my speech does have traces of pomposity. And now, if I may comment on your own mode of speech, I am intrigued by your choice of the word "useful." *Why* would I find it useful to invent Ostos' last words?

SEVIGNE   Because for some days before the crime, Ostos suspected you. Furthermore, you knew it.

JOSEFA   He didn't know it. I knew it, but Monsieur Beaurevers did not.

BEAUREVERS   Ah ... there you are.

SEVIGNE   We'll see.
        (*He reaches for the file on his desk.* JOSEFA *winces*)

JOSEFA   (*Whispered, to* BEAUREVERS)   Watch out for that book —it's loaded!
        (*At a glare from* SEVIGNE, *she subsides*)

SEVIGNE   Now, then . . . (*Rising, addressing* BEAUREVERS *formally*) I refer to a conversation you had with Madame Marthe Herbeux—

BEAUREVERS   Who?

JOSEFA   The cook—Camel-face.

SEVIGNE (*Annoyed*) —a few days before the shooting she warned you to stop your affair with Josefa Lantenay. She warned you that Ostos suspected what was going on— (BEAUREVERS *looks at him, impassive*)—and you replied: "What can I do, Marthe? I can't give her up—she's in my blood."

JOSEFA (*Enchanted*) Me? In *your* blood? What an honor!
(BEAUREVERS *is troubled, and seeing his concern,* JOSEFA'S *pleasure vanishes. She watches and listens closely*)

SEVIGNE Well?

BEAUREVERS (*Carefully*) It does not seem to be an entirely characteristic remark for me to make, does it?

SEVIGNE Are you denying that you made it?

BEAUREVERS No . . . it's just that I can't remember.

SEVIGNE If I read more of that conversation . . . (*Opening the file*) . . . perhaps your memory will improve?

BEAUREVERS You can try, but quite candidly, I doubt it.

JOSEFA Monsieur Beaurevers has a terrible memory! He forgets dates, names, places—everything . . .

SEVIGNE Charming, isn't it? The girl is accused of murder, and all she thinks about is how to defend you.

BEAUREVERS Yes, I find it touching and beautiful. Thank you, Josefa.

JOSEFA (*Embarrassed*) It's nothing.

BEAUREVERS No, my dear Josefa, it is something very special which I shall always remember.
(*They are getting lost in each other once more and* SEVIGNE *taps sharply with his pencil*)

SEVIGNE Please, no tripping over roots here. (*And as* BEAU-REVERS *turns back to him*) The cook also told you that Ostos had been brandishing a knife, and you told her not to worry ... (*Consulting the file*) And I quote: "A knife is a romantic but outmoded weapon in terms of modern armament, especially if opposed by a gun."

BEAUREVERS (*Reluctantly*) I admit, that *sounds* like me.

JOSEFA (*Quickly*) It's ridiculous—can you imagine Monsieur Beaurevers in that kind of conversation with a cook?

SEVIGNE Shut up!

JOSEFA (*Carrying on desperately*) And besides, there were no witnesses.

SEVIGNE Another word, and I'll throw you out!

BEAUREVERS (*Calmly*) Just the same, an excellent point has been made—no witnesses.

SEVIGNE If it's witnesses you want, then I will refer to your conversation at the Volney Club with Monsieur Guillaume Ancenis. (*He has whipped out some pages of testimony*) You confided in Monsieur Ancenis that you loved a certain "Jo-Jo." You didn't tell him that your "Jo-Jo" was also your maid, but you did say—(*Brandishing the paper*) "To keep her I would be capable of anything. Even a divorce. *Even a crime.*"

BEAUREVERS Oh, that son of a bitch!
    (BEAUREVERS *is plainly taken aback*)

SEVIGNE Splendid! Your speech is much simpler now. The bartender and two other members have verified this conversation.

71

BEAUREVERS (*Bitterly*) That's club life for you nowadays!

SEVIGNE Is your memory improving?

BEAUREVERS I remember something like that conversation . . .

SEVIGNE Congratulations!

BEAUREVERS (*Grudgingly*) Those damn witnesses! A private conversation—*in my club*. And I can't even resign; I bought a life membership!
(JOSEFA *is alert to the danger of this testimony*)

JOSEFA It was nothing but talk—loose talk. He was probably on his seventh whiskey—

BEAUREVERS Josefa! Be still! (*He studies* SEVIGNE *as if measuring the menace*) Are you implying that I killed Ostos?

SEVIGNE (*Casually*) Well, let's see how it shapes up, shall we? A charge of murder, to be sustained, consists of three major elements: motive, opportunity, premeditation. Your conversations with the cook and at the club provide a motive; opportunity certainly existed; and premeditation may be assumed if you arranged to be alone in the house—

BEAUREVERS What I had in mind was not murder.

SEVIGNE In addition, you were the first to appear at the scene of the crime—

BEAUREVERS Please bear in mind: *after* the crime.

SEVIGNE True . . . but if you had arranged matters that way . . .
(*He lets the accusation trail off*)

JOSEFA (*Shocked*) Oh!

BEAUREVERS (*With great dignity*) It is just such innuendo and insinuation that make a hollow mockery of justice in our times. (*Rising*) I wish you good day.

SEVIGNE (*Mildly*) Good day. (*And then*) I think you'll find that Madame Beaurevers is still waiting in that corridor—
(BEAUREVERS *stops, turns, comes back to his chair*)

SEVIGNE Thank you.

BEAUREVERS A man caught between a prosecutor and his wife has little or no choice. (*Facing* SEVIGNE) Continue.

SEVIGNE Normally, the cook would have been in the house that night, but you bribed her to go out.

JOSEFA That cook—with a mouth bigger than her oven!

SEVIGNE (*Turning on her*) Oh—*you* again. Do you know the penalty for perjury?

JOSEFA Perjury?

SEVIGNE Lying!

JOSEFA (*Relieved*) Oh—lying. (*Eagerly, smiling*) But I don't mean any harm when I do it—

SEVIGNE (*From the file*) Josefa Lantenay, in your interrogation two days ago, you were asked the following question: "On the night of the crime, did you have any visitors other than Miguel Ostos?" You evaded the question by jabbering about everything under the sun but when you were finally forced to reply you said: "No!" (*Snaps the file shut with a thump*) Do you now want to change your answer?

JOSEFA (*Weakly*) No.

SEVIGNE One more chance: Did you have any other visitors?

JOSEFA (*Rising*) Send me back to prison!

SEVIGNE (*Furious*) Sit down!

JOSEFA I insist.

BEAUREVERS (*Quietly*) Answer the question, Josefa.

JOSEFA (*Startled*) What? Oh, no—
  (*There is a long pause*)

SEVIGNE It seems to have answered itself—thank you.
  (JOSEFA *sinks back into her chair*)

BEAUREVERS We were together that night—from eight o'clock until ten. My wife was visiting friends; it was a simple matter to get rid of the cook for the evening; and Ostos was sent on an errand to our branch bank in Lyons.

SEVIGNE Yes, that is confirmed by the police.

BEAUREVERS *I'm* a fast driver, and I could not have been back before midnight, at the earliest. It's utter madness that he was home at eleven. I would have sworn it was impossible.

SEVIGNE I'll bet you were surprised to see him.

BEAUREVERS Eh? (*He looks thoughtfully at* SEVIGNE) Ah, yes, I see what you mean. You're suggesting that he found us together.

SEVIGNE (*Matter of fact*) A jealous rage . . . Ostos was famous for those, wasn't he? He attacked you, and you fired in legitimate self-defense.

BEAUREVERS (*Dryly*) Is that a firm offer?

SEVIGNE (*In the same tone*) I can't give it to you in writing.

BEAUREVERS It won't be necessary. I left Josefa at ten o'clock.

JOSEFA (*Instantly*)   True. Ten o'clock on the dot. (*As* SEVIGNE *looks at her*) I heard the clock striking, and I looked at my watch.

SEVIGNE   Why ten o'clock—since you believed Ostos couldn't be back until after midnight?

BEAUREVERS   Unfortunately, my wife's arrival could not be as accurately predicted. (*Delicately*) Besides . . . eight to ten— one is no longer in the first fine flush of youth . . . (*Turning to* MORESTAN) My dear fellow, without prejudice to the investigation, you might omit that last remark.

JOSEFA   Besides, it's not true.

BEAUREVERS   Thank you, Josefa.

SEVIGNE (*Musing*)   Eight to ten . . . and well out of the way before anything happened to Ostos. You had another plan to meet that night, didn't you?

JOSEFA   No.

BEAUREVERS (*Simultaneously*)   Yes.

SEVIGNE   At eleven o'clock? The time Ostos was shot?

JOSEFA   No.

BEAUREVERS (*Simultaneously*)   Yes.

SEVIGNE   Surely, what you had in mind takes two?

BEAUREVERS   We had planned to meet at eleven o'clock. I sent Josefa a note telling her so.

JOSEFA   No—I never got it—it's not true.
   (*Both* BEAUREVERS *and* SEVIGNE *take it for granted that she is only defending her lover, as before*)

75

BEAUREVERS   Let us not confuse each other—over trifles, my dear—

JOSEFA   But I didn't get the note—I knew nothing about meeting at eleven—

SEVIGNE   (*Wrathfully*)   Out! (*Pointing*) Morestan, call the guard and ask him to—

JOSEFA   No, no. I won't interrupt again. I swear it.
(SEVIGNE *subsides, nodding to* MORESTAN)

BEAUREVERS   You see, the chauffeur was already out of the way ... my wife decided to stay with her friends for dinner ... (*With a shrug and a smile*) Why grow old waiting?

SEVIGNE   Why, indeed. (*And then*) Your conversations with the cook, and at the club, those indicate quite a degree of feeling, don't they?

JOSEFA   I tell you he must have been drinking.

BEAUREVERS   All right, Josefa. That's enough. It's not important.

JOSEFA   It is. He's accusing you! Tell him!

SEVIGNE   Actually, Monsieur Beaurevers is accusing himself— (*Holding a document*) "To keep her I would be capable of anything. Even a divorce. Even a crime." *Is* that how you feel?

JOSEFA   (*To* SEVIGNE)   No, it isn't. I'm like that! You said so yourself! But him—*never!*

SEVIGNE   (*To* BEAUREVERS, *formally*)   I think it's time you spoke for yourself. How *do* you feel?

76

BEAUREVERS (*Quietly*) This is how: I have a brutal, raging need of her. She *is* in my blood, like a fever that sets me trembling. (SEVIGNE *is surprised, a little embarrassed by the outburst;* JOSEFA *is puzzled, too worried, momentarily, to really understand what he is saying*) It's a craving. I'm addicted to her. When I'm deprived of the relief that only she can give me, a dull aching pain settles in the back of my skull, and throbs there, hammering at me. (JOSEFA *looks confused, frightened*) But I don't love her! I feel nothing for her except my need of her. Is that love! Is an addict in love with his heroin or cocaine?

JOSEFA (*Hurt*) No—don't say it—please!

BEAUREVERS I must. (*He turns his back on* JOSEFA, *facing* SEVIGNE) I don't care what you think or what you suspect. I'm saying this to break the relationship, to be free. Do you think I would kill Ostos . . . divorce my wife . . . and then what? Live with her—torn between her embarrassed silence and insane, explosive jealousy? To be perpetually at the mercy of her mood? No! No, thank you! In time, I think, I could have killed. But only one of us. Josefa or myself. That at least would buy me back my freedom, but killing Ostos to have her for myself—that meant slavery.

JOSEFA (*After a silence*) I want very much to faint . . . very much . . .
   (*She sways a bit, but that's all*)

SEVIGNE (*To* BEAUREVERS) Well, your relationship is clarified, I guess . . .

JOSEFA (*Shivering*) It's cold here . . .

BEAUREVERS I had to do it. (*Without looking at her*) I'm sorry, Josefa.

77

JOSEFA   Miguel, at least, only hit me with his fist.

BEAUREVERS (*To* SEVIGNE)   Can I go now?

SEVIGNE   In a moment. Just let me—(*His telephone rings*) Damn! (*Snatches it, irritably*) Sevigne speaking—(*And in an entirely different tone*) Yes, sir. Yes, thank you, sir, I'll be delighted to have your opinion. (*Helplessly*) Go right ahead, sir.

> (*He listens impatiently, not daring to interrupt, fidgeting and twisting in his chair*)

JOSEFA (*To* BEAUREVERS)   I was ashamed of my ignorance . . . I used to wish that you'd speak simply, so I could understand . . . (*With a deep sigh*) Well, finally! (*At his unbending back*) Turn around . . . you used to swallow me with your eyes. At least look at me now!

> (SEVIGNE, *listening, gestures frantically for silence*)

JOSEFA   Liar! (*And then, wounded*) Does an addict love his drug? Now, that's a pretty speech I'll always remember!

SEVIGNE (*Into the telephone*)   No, sir, I didn't say *anything*. I have some people here and—(*Then resigned again*) Yes, sir, I'm listening.

> (*And he does*)

JOSEFA   I wanted you to need me . . . the way I needed you . . . not on prescription, like a pain-killer. Forgive me for the headaches I gave you. And if I meant so much to you, forgive me for that, too. (*Softly, deeply hurt*) And for having pleased you so much! (*And then, angrily*) My God, what lies! Liar! Liar!

> (SEVIGNE *gestures frantically for silence*)

SEVIGNE (*Into the telephone*)   No, sir, I didn't say anything. I'm listening.

JOSEFA (*Steaming*) You used to whisper that I gave you wings ... you said my body was a launching pad for a rocket of dreams. What kind of a drug is *that?* You've gotten rid of that dull aching pain at the back of the skull, haven't you? I've got it now. You gave it to me.

SEVIGNE (*Covering the mouthpiece*) Stop it—I can't hear— (*Into the telephone*) Yes, sir, that's my opinion, too—

JOSEFA (*Going right on*) The village idiot, that's me. I believed everything. (*Mimicking*) "My wife doesn't understand me." Nobody believes that any more. And I believed it. (*Mimicking*) "I need you, Josefa. My wife and I live like brother and sister. And I have nobody." And I believed even that. I *knew* it was a lie, and I believed it.

SEVIGNE A little less noise if you please! I am talking to the Chief Prosecutor. (*And into the telephone*) Yes, sir, I'm listening.
> (*He is torn, in fact, as* JOSEFA *continues her tirade, between listening to the Chief and to what she is saying*)

JOSEFA (*Bitterly*) Those poker games that went on all night at your club! How many times I lay weeping at your lies and heard you creeping into the house, tiptoeing upstairs to *her.*
> (BEAUREVERS *has stiffened like a ramrod at this. He wheels around slowly, like a piece of heavy artillery*)

JOSEFA Sneaking up the stairs ... (*With utter contempt*) ... to your wife.

BEAUREVERS (*Oddly strained*) What are you saying?

JOSEFA Liar! And what a cheap, stupid lie! Do you deny it? Just last week—Tuesday—another all-night game—but before midnight you were creeping up the stairs—to her.

BEAUREVERS (*With some difficulty*) Tuesday—I played until seven o'clock in the morning. I lost twenty thousand francs. *New* francs.

JOSEFA Stop it! I heard your key in the lock . . . then your footsteps, quietly, going upstairs . . .
  (*The look on* BEAUREVERS' *face puzzles her*)

BEAUREVERS (*Hoarse*) Who was it? Who was the man?

JOSEFA (*Uncertain now*) It was you . . . who else could open the front door with a key . . . every time you had an all-night poker game. (*And then, horrified by what she has revealed*) Oh!

BEAUREVERS Dominique!

SEVIGNE (*Into the telephone, frantically*) Chief, if I could call you back . . . I think there is an important development . . . (*And then frustrated, listening*) Yes, sir.

BEAUREVERS Dominique! (*He slowly massages the back of his skull*) My wife! . . . My head! (*Weakly, to* JOSEFA) Every time I played poker? . . . You're sure? (*And then, a groan*) Dominique!

SEVIGNE (*Into the telephone*) Yes, sir, of course, I know what the Beaurevers family stands for . . . (*He listens*) Madame Beaurevers, too—yes, sir . . . (*Glancing up at* BEAUREVERS) His position? Yes, sir . . . (BEAUREVERS *is massaging his skull again, slowly, painfully*) I particularly know what he stands for . . . (*Thoughtfully*) So does he.
  (*It has taken* JOSEFA *a few moments to realize that this is her revenge, and she breaks suddenly into wild laughter*)

Curtain

Julie Harris, William Shatner, and Walter Matthau,
as JOSEFA, SEVIGNE, and BENJAMIN BEAUREVERS

ACT THREE

It is the same day, between five and six P.M.

At rise, SEVIGNE *is seated at his desk and* MORESTAN *is, as usual, facing him across the room.* LABLACHE *is pacing, which is not easy in the remaining space, but he is doing the best he can. The atmosphere is strained.*

LABLACHE (*Finally*) Really! I must say, Sevigne, that you surprise me. Forty-eight hours ago I gave you an assignment about as innocent of repercussions as a grocer charged with blocking the sidewalk. Two days—two little days—and suddenly we have something like the Dreyfus case on our hands. You are pursuing a very dangerous course.

SEVIGNE Do I have any choice?

LABLACHE All right—let's examine the revised situation. It would appear that you have uncovered some indiscretion on the part of Madame Beaurevers—

SEVIGNE She had a lover.

LABLACHE Horrible! Nobody in Paris would believe such a thing!

SEVIGNE I didn't find the news overwhelming, but the husband involved—well, you should have seen Beaurevers when it hit him!

LABLACHE And for that very reason, I urge you not to believe too much. Husbands—even wives, in such circumstances— are notoriously vindictive.

SEVIGNE I'm aware of that.

LABLACHE Furthermore, to conclude that such a situation inevitably leads to murder is sheer insanity. My God, if that were true, you'd hear nothing but gunfire all day long and the streets of Paris would be choked with funeral processions.

SEVIGNE I draw no conclusions. I prefer that you judge the testimony for yourself.

LABLACHE (*Reluctantly*) All right.

SEVIGNE (*To* MORESTAN) Ready?

MORESTAN Yes, sir. (*Clears his throat importantly. At* SEVIGNE's *gesture he starts to read from his notes. He reads slowly, clearly and distinctly, in a monotone, with no expression whatever*) Question: "Are you now prepared to make a new statement?" Answer: "Yes. I want to settle with that bitch."

LABLACHE What?

MORESTAN Excuse me, I'm only reading.

LABLACHE He used that word?

SEVIGNE His speech became surprisingly colloquial. (*To* MORESTAN) Go on.

MORESTAN (*Reading*) "It was not I who first reached the scene of the crime—it was my wife."

LABLACHE What? Does he explain his original statement?

SEVIGNE Go on, Morestan.

MORESTAN Question: "Why did you previously state that you were the first to arrive?" Answer: "It was my wife's idea."

LABLACHE (*Skeptically*) Ha!
  (MORESTAN *gives him a reproving look*)

MORESTAN Question: "Why did you agree to this if it was not true?" Answer: "I was completely bewildered and I had complete confidence in Dominique. Besides, I thought that if I said I was the first, I could help Josefa by suppressing the statement Dominique told me Ostos made when he was dying, in which he accused Josefa of the shooting."

LABLACHE (*Pained, grudgingly*) Is that true?

SEVIGNE Inspector Colas confirms that Beaurevers withheld that information until it was dropped by Madame.
(*And as* LABLACHE *groans, he gestures to* MORESTAN *to continue*)

MORESTAN Question: "What did *you* see when you entered the room?" Answer: "My wife bending over Josefa, who was unconscious on the floor. I believed what she told me then—that Josefa had killed her lover, but I think now that she was just putting the revolver in Josefa's hand."

LABLACHE (*Hoping against hope*) As I warned you, the words of a vindictive husband.
(*At a sign from* SEVIGNE, MORESTAN *picks up the narration*)

MORESTAN Question: "Ostos was much taller than you. How is it possible that your wife could have mistaken him for you?"

LABLACHE (*Warmly*) Ah, an excellent point.

MORESTAN Answer: "It was due to modesty." Question: "Whose modesty?" Answer: "Ostos' modesty. The room was in total darkness. My wife fired at a shadow she thought was mine. Poor Ostos, if he were at all like me, he would be alive today, because in such circumstances *I* like to see what I'm doing." (*Apologetically to* LABLACHE) Excuse me—I'm only reading.

LABLACHE Go on!

MORESTAN "But for Ostos' modesty, my wife would now be a rich, beautiful, young widow. A decent interval of mourning —Dominique looks marvelous in black, by the way—and she would be free to marry her lover." Question: "Who is the man?" Answer: "Monsieur Jean-Claude de Benoit, one thirty-nine rue de Varenne, Paris, Seventh Arrondissement. Telephone: Invalides two eight nine three." Question: "How is it that you're so certain?" Answer: "He is my best friend."

SEVIGNE Charming lot, your Beaurevers!

LABLACHE They are not my Beaurevers. And so far, what they've done is not illegal—it's not even unpopular. (*Curtly, to* MORESTAN) Go on.

MORESTAN (*Reading*) Question: "There is no doubt in your mind that Monsieur de Benoit is the man?" Answer: "None whatever. He and my wife were inseparable due to their mutual passion for horses—or so I thought. He spent all the holidays with us at Hauterive—hunting, riding, racing. Now I remember how many times, when they came back from the trails, *they* were exhausted, and the horses were fresh." Question: "Do you now formally accuse your wife of murdering Ostos?" Answer: "I do."

SEVIGNE Well, that's certainly illegal, and probably unpopular.

LABLACHE She makes the same accusation against him, doesn't she?

SEVIGNE He adds a few details, some of them quite convincing. The gloves, Morestan.

MORESTAN Coming up. (*He riffles the pages of his book to find the appropriate page, then, locating it, clears his throat*)

Question: "Do you actually believe that your wife planned a cold-blooded, premeditated murder?" Answer: "Ha!" (*Apologetically, to* LABLACHE) H-A, and an exclamation. (*And then from his notes*) Question: "Can you be more precise?" Answer: "She got the note I intended for Josefa, and she expected to find me in the room. Furthermore, I call to your attention that she was still wearing her gloves, so that her fingerprints would not appear on the gun or anywhere in the room."

LABLACHE In the police interrogation did he not mention that she was wearing her gloves?

SEVIGNE No.

MORESTAN Question: "Why did you withhold this information from the police?" Answer: "Because it didn't seem important." Question: "Why does it seem important now?" Answer: "When a wife has a lover, *all* her actions seem more important."

LABLACHE (*Involuntarily*) God knows, that's true! (*And then*) But it has no legal bearing whatsoever. I'm sure she had reasonable explanations for everything. Didn't she?

SEVIGNE She was fantastically good. Poised, calm, serene—sat there like Whistler's mother, dressed by Balenciaga. Then suddenly a tiny crack in that glossy surface—
(*With a gesture to* MORESTAN, *who reads*)

MORESTAN Question: "Did you wear gloves that night, Madame?"

SEVIGNE This was followed by a terrible silence.

MORESTAN I made a note. Silence. Then, finally, answer: "It's possible. I had just come in from outdoors. I heard the shot and it's possible that I didn't pause to take off my gloves."

SEVIGNE Now she suddenly realized that her husband had talked.

MORESTAN Question: "You seem pale, Madame. Would you like a glass of water?" Answer: "No. If I am pale, it is because of the strain on me, but I can no longer conceal the truth. I love my husband, whatever his shortcomings, but I have endured too much ..."

SEVIGNE Here her voice broke, and very reluctantly, she told *her* story. Read us that tender chapter in the home life of the Beaurevers family, Morestan.

MORESTAN Question: "On entering the room, what did you see?" Answer: "Ostos was lying dead on the floor and my husband was on his knees beside Josefa. At my entrance, he gave a wild cry of alarm, like some trapped animal. I was terrified. And in my panic, with his frenzied pleadings in my ears, I became his accomplice. I was *not* wearing my gloves, but he used them to wipe the fingerprints from the weapon, then he put it in Josefa's hand."

LABLACHE God, you read badly!

MORESTAN (*Defensively*) I'm a clerk; I read like a clerk.

SEVIGNE Perhaps you'd like to hear what went on when they were finally face to face?

LABLACHE No, no—spare me. (*He gets up, paces around nervously again, then timidly*) They—they actually repeated their accusations then?

SEVIGNE Savagely. They shouted unprintable things at one another. Monstrous accusations. And then—(*Producing two documents with seals affixed*)—they signed them.

LABLACHE (*Utter unenthusiasm*) Good work! Splendid! Identical confessions . . . they accuse each other . . . not very conclusive, is it?

SEVIGNE Not so far.
(LABLACHE *has a thoughtful moment*)

LABLACHE Er—Morestan, would you mind stepping over to the Second Tribunal and waiting for the verdict in the Trevillon case? Let me know what happens.

MORESTAN Yes, sir.
(*He goes.* LABLACHE *starts pacing again,* SEVIGNE *watching him*)

LABLACHE We want to give this some thought, don't we? (*And as* SEVIGNE *nods*) Ostos is dead . . . the girl is unconscious . . . (*Ticking them off on two fingers*) The husband and wife accuse each other and, generally speaking, that cancels their testimony. Result—*no* witnesses.

SEVIGNE That's true.

LABLACHE (*Indicating the* BEAUREVERS' *statements*) How much of all this does Josefa Lantenay know?

SEVIGNE So far, nothing.

LABLACHE (*Gratified*) Ah! . . . (*Wistfully*) But she has a lawyer now, hasn't she?

SEVIGNE I assigned one, but she wouldn't see him or have anything to do with him.

LABLACHE (*Casually*) How do you plan to proceed?

SEVIGNE (*Just as casually*) To begin with, we might as well let the girl go.

LABLACHE Hm-m-m—

SEVIGNE That is the first step, isn't it?

LABLACHE If you release the girl, the case explodes at once. (*At* SEVIGNE's *shrug*) The newspapers are whispering already. With the girl cleared, they'd roar.

SEVIGNE I suppose so—yes.

LABLACHE Scandal is mud. Give it time to dry and it turns to dust. Then deal with it.

SEVIGNE To protect the Beaurevers?

LABLACHE Yes, damn it! Oh, I know it isn't equal justice under law, but the Beaurevers just aren't equal. Condemn me if you like—I'm afraid of them.

SEVIGNE (*Troubled*) So am I.

LABLACHE (*Ingenuously*) And what's the harm, finally? If this case remains an affair of a chauffeur and a maid, I give you my word that in two months' time it won't matter to anyone.

SEVIGNE Except, of course, to the maid.

LABLACHE In the long run, even she'll be better off without a scandal trailing along behind her.

SEVIGNE (*Thoughtfully*) Lablache, have you ever been in a women's prison?

LABLACHE (*Surprised*) Eh? Why?

SEVIGNE Oh, I just wondered what you thought of conditions in them?

LABLACHE (*Nettled*) No, I have not been in a women's prison. (*Pointedly*) Also, I am not a parlormaid who sleeps with the Spanish chauffeur *and* her boss. Wake up, Sevigne—the girl isn't so much of an ingénue that you must act like a juvenile.

SEVIGNE (*Thoughtfully*) Two months, you say? ...

LABLACHE Not even that. Six weeks.

SEVIGNE Six weeks? (*And then*) No, damn it, I can't!

LABLACHE A month.

SEVIGNE No! Not one day! Why should the girl pay for the Beaurevers? Because they're so much richer than she is?
(LABLACHE *nods resignedly*)

LABLACHE You'll be finished today?

SEVIGNE Are you asking me?—Or telling me? (LABLACHE *shrugs*) I hope to be finished today—yes.

LABLACHE Well, then, that's that. (*And then, shrewdly*) In coming to a decision, have you thought of your wife? (*At* SEVIGNE's *glance*) I mean, she is involved in your future, isn't she?

SEVIGNE Yes, very much so. (*And then, stoutly*) Whatever I do, I know I can count on Antoinette.

LABLACHE Ah, well, you're a lucky man ... (*He starts out, pausing before he goes*) Good luck then, Sevigne—*with everything.*
(*He exits*)

SEVIGNE Lablache! (SEVIGNE, *left alone, doesn't seem quite so sure of himself. A couple of times he reaches for the phone and then pulls back as though unwilling to make the test, but finally he takes it, dials a number*) Hello ... Antoinette? ... How are you, darling? ... No, I'm fine. ... I had a few minutes between chores and I wanted to talk to you. . . . The case? . . . Well, I think it's going very well, but there seems to be a difference of opinion . . . (*He braces himself for a moment*) . . . I may be taken off it before the day is over. (*He listens, smiling for the first time*) The Chief Prosecutor is a *what*? (*Delighted*) Antoinette, where did you ever learn such a word? (*Then, crestfallen*) Oh, that's what your mother used to call *me*? (*Then, soberly*) Antoinette, what if your mother were right . . . I mean, if things were rough for a while: no new apartment, or car—(*He smiles then, listening, and his smile becomes wider and wider, and he says softly*) Thank you, darling. Goodbye.

(*He puts down the phone. His dejection is gone. He turns back to his desk and the work as* MORESTAN *enters*)

MORESTAN   Lablache is gone? You seem pretty cheerful.

SEVIGNE   We'd better get back to work. Lablache implied that if I wanted to finish on this case, I'd better work fast.

MORESTAN   Yes, that's the rumor in the building. The girl is waiting. Want her?

SEVIGNE   How is she behaving?

MORESTAN   Hard to tell. She's sound asleep on a bench.

SEVIGNE   It seems to be a lot less strain on her than on me. Yes, get her in. (MORESTAN *goes out, returning in a moment with* JOSEFA. *She is rubbing her eyes, as if from a sleep, and she looks around the office eagerly, apparently a bit let down at finding herself alone with the two men*) Expecting someone?

JOSEFA   No . . .
      (*She seems very subdued*)

SEVIGNE Sit down.

(She takes the indicated chair, folding her coat over the back. Once or twice she seems about to speak, doesn't quite make it. Then, finally:)

JOSEFA Monsieur has gone?

SEVIGNE Monsieur?

JOSEFA Monsieur Beaurevers? (*And then a groan*) My big mouth: I'm even worse than the cook! (*Plaintively*) And he *was* playing poker all night long. Does telling the truth ever help *anybody?*

SEVIGNE In my official capacity I don't think I ought to answer that.

JOSEFA He was terribly upset, wasn't he?

SEVIGNE Reasonably. (*He watches her. She is nervous, fidgeting, bracing herself for something*) What's wrong with you?

JOSEFA Nothing—now. It's over. I want to confess.

SEVIGNE What!

JOSEFA I'm just not bright enough to keep track of all my lies. The strain is too much. I want to confess.

SEVIGNE Anything special?

JOSEFA I killed Miguel. (MORESTAN *drops his pen, with an exclamation. She turns to him*) Write! Take it down! (*As* MORESTAN *stares at her*) You've been writing down even my sneezes for two days, and suddenly you're helpless. *I'm confessing!*

SEVIGNE Here—look at me! (*She turns, warily*) Why are you being such an idiot?

JOSEFA A conscience that jabs me like a red-hot spear—you call that idiotic?

SEVIGNE If you're still protecting Monsieur Beaurevers, let me tell you—

JOSEFA Protecting *him?* After what you heard him say to me in this room?

SEVIGNE All right. Go on. Take it, Morestan.

JOSEFA Thank you. (*She braces herself*) I killed Miguel . . . I shot him . . . with the pistol kept in the Rolls-Royce—

SEVIGNE Which Rolls-Royce?

JOSEFA The limousine.

SEVIGNE Go on.

JOSEFA I shot him. . . . Of course, I didn't mean to kill him—only to wound him—but there you are—(*She is running out of steam; plaintively*) Don't you want to ask me any questions?

SEVIGNE And interrupt you in the middle of your confession?

JOSEFA I don't mind.

SEVIGNE Well, *why* did you kill him?

JOSEFA Ah! (*She is ready for this one*) His brutality. He beat me. You know that from witnesses, don't you? Well, that night again, because he was suspicious—

SEVIGNE You had no bruises . . .

JOSEFA He held me by the hair and beat my head against the floor. That's how I got this bump. I thought he meant to kill me. So I fired. (*Glances to see if* MORESTAN *has it all, then sighs*) I feel better now.

SEVIGNE Where was the revolver?

JOSEFA When I shot him—in my hand, of course.

SEVIGNE No—I mean, where did you have it in your room? (*As she looks at him unhappily*) In a drawer? . . . In your purse? . . . In the bed? . . . Under the bed?

JOSEFA (*Eagerly*) Under the bed. I reached for it. I hardly knew what I was doing, he was giving me such a thumping—

SEVIGNE The shot was fired from a distance of at least ten feet.

JOSEFA I—I—I broke away from him—(*Inspiration*) The gun was under the other side of the bed.

SEVIGNE How did it get there?

JOSEFA We struggled for it . . . I knocked it out of his hand . . . it fell to the floor and—I kicked it. (MORESTAN *is listening open-mouthed. She adds plaintively*) He's not writing anything!

SEVIGNE All right, Morestan. Take it down, just as she told it. There is no longer any case against Madame Beaurevers.

JOSEFA (*Humbly*) I'm sorry I didn't confess right away. (*Then it hits her*) Madame Beaurevers! I thought it was *him*.

SEVIGNE (*Severely*) That's none of your business. Go on with your confession. (*And as* JOSEFA *hesitates in painful uncertainty*) Where's that red-hot spear of conscience that was jabbing you a minute ago?

JOSEFA It sort of comes and goes. . . . (*Looks pleadingly at* SEVIGNE) What's this about Madame?

SEVIGNE (*Tinged with pity*) Idiot!

JOSEFA (*Humbly*) I know.

SEVIGNE It seems that it was Madame Beaurevers who was first in the room after the shooting. *She* found you?

JOSEFA (*Embarrassed*) Madame? (*She tugs her skirt down*) But *he* heard Miguel accuse me ... his last words ... (*And as* SEVIGNE *shakes his head; delighted*) Oh! (*Impulsively she takes his hand, kisses it. Surprised,* SEVIGNE *backs away from her quickly*) Then he *didn't* die thinking I shot him! Oh, thank you! Thank you for that! (*Then suddenly wounded*) Monsieur Beaurevers used that against me—

SEVIGNE He thought it was true. It was his wife who said she heard Ostos accuse you.

JOSEFA (*Delighted again, looking up*) Miguel, do you hear? Are you listening, my poor Miguel? (*To* SEVIGNE) Do you think he *is* listening somewhere ... do you think he knows now that I'm innocent?

SEVIGNE (*Kindly*) Perhaps. I hope so.

JOSEFA Innocent or not, if he could get his hands on me right now, I'd get a good clip on the ear. (*Looking up*) Forgive me, Miguel. I should have known it was you who really loved me.

SEVIGNE When you've finished with the spirit world, I'd like to get back to business.

JOSEFA Did she kill Miguel? (*Awed, rocking in surprise and a touch of admiration*) That crazy Spaniard? He and Madame—*also*?

SEVIGNE No.

JOSEFA (*Skeptically*) They weren't—not *anything?*

SEVIGNE She expected to find her husband in your room.

JOSEFA (*Shocked*) Oh! (*Wincing*) Poor Miguel! He died by mistake—like a wrong number! (*Impulsively, passionately*) Punish her! Put her in prison! She can have my room!

SEVIGNE Well—

JOSEFA You must. (*Earnestly*) Miguel must be avenged. To a Spaniard these things are terribly important. You must punish her! I'm not asking for myself—for Miguel. I'll help you.

SEVIGNE Thank you. That's just what I need. You deny everything, you confess everything. You're really a big help!

JOSEFA I'm sorry. But please let me help—

SEVIGNE Shut up, I'm thinking. . . . Do you know her wardrobe?

JOSEFA Yes.

SEVIGNE Everything?

JOSEFA Everything—even her underwear. Do you want me to search her?

SEVIGNE Stop babbling! (*Pointing to a corner*) Sit over there.

JOSEFA Yes, sir.
(*She goes obediently to her corner*)

SEVIGNE Sit still, and listen.
(*When she is settled he nods to* MORESTAN, *who rises and goes to the door, admitting* MADAME BEAUREVERS. *She makes her accustomed sweeping entrance*)

97

MADAME BEAUREVERS Well, at last!

SEVIGNE (*Who has risen politely*) I'm sorry to have kept you waiting. Please sit down.

MADAME BEAUREVERS (*Graciously*) Thank you. (*And in turning*) Ah, Josefa! (*Looking her up and down*) I must say, prison seems to agree with you.

JOSEFA Thank you, Madame. (*Pointedly*) It's possible to get used to anything.

SEVIGNE And now, Madame, there are a few questions I would like to clear up.

MADAME BEAUREVERS Very well.
    (*She sits*)

SEVIGNE Who is Monsieur Jean-Claude de Benoit?

MADAME BEAUREVERS A childhood friend.

SEVIGNE (*Mildly*) Children grow up . . . they learn new games . . . (JOSEFA *is gesturing as with a sword:* "*Attack, attack!*" SEVIGNE *has whisked a paper deftly from the file*) Three months ago, when you returned from the country, you yourself ordered a new key to the front door of your house. (*And as the witness's composure is momentarily bruised*) Why?

MADAME BEAUREVERS I—I had lost mine . . . I wanted to replace it.

SEVIGNE (*From the paper*) But the locksmith swears—(*Rattling the paper*)—that you had your key; that in fact you gave it to him so that he could copy it. *Why?*

MADAME BEAUREVERS I must have wanted—needed—a duplicate.

SEVIGNE Where it is now?

MADAME BEAUREVERS I don't know. I may have misplaced it. (*Gathering anger*) Really! It seems to be a great fuss about nothing at all.

SEVIGNE Yes, of course. Childhood friends! Nothing more natural than that Monsieur de Benoit should have a key of his own and come and go as he pleased.

MADAME BEAUREVERS (*Indifferently*) Think what you like. It is of no importance.

SEVIGNE I am content that you should be the judge of that, Madame. However, we are investigating a murder, and this bears directly on your own motive.

JOSEFA (*Explosively*) Ole! Ole! (SEVIGNE *glares at her and* MADAME BEAUREVERS *turns slowly;* JOSEFA *subsides*) I—I was thinking of something else . . . excuse me.

MADAME BEAUREVERS Thinking of something else! Does she *ever* think of anything else? Frankly, then: my husband and this unwashed rabbit were carrying on—under my own roof, humiliating me before my own servants. Very well. I found a means of consolation. You may investigate it, if you like, until doomsday.

SEVIGNE I think we can drop the matter. (JOSEFA *seems pained*) Except for one minor point. (JOSEFA *brightens*) Do you have money of your own, Madame?

MADAME BEAUREVERS (*Stiffly*) Really! I am not considering opening an account here, you know. . . . (*And under* SE-VIGNE's *steady, waiting stare*) We are a very old and, if I may say so, distinguished family. Not merchants or bankers.

99

SEVIGNE In other words, you are dependent on Monsieur Beaurevers . . . (*She shrugs it off*) You knew from the servants' gossip, did you not, that your husband visited Josefa from time to time?

(JOSEFA *looks demure, tugging down her skirt*)

MADAME BEAUREVERS (*Contemptuously*) Yes, of course.

SEVIGNE Did you know when?

MADAME BEAUREVERS No.

SEVIGNE In the early afternoon on the day of the shooting, your husband sent Josefa a note fixing a rendezvous for ten o'clock that night. She never got the note. Do you know anything about that, Madame?

MADAME BEAUREVERS Nothing whatever.

SEVIGNE You dined with friends that night?

MADAME BEAUREVERS Yes. Monsieur and Madame Belvoir.

SEVIGNE Was that a long-standing invitation?

MADAME BEAUREVERS No . . . actually it was arranged that same day.

SEVIGNE Was it at their suggestion . . . or yours?

MADAME BEAUREVERS I—I don't remember. We are very old friends—what possible difference can it make?

SEVIGNE (*Gently*) If you *had* intercepted your husband's note, and knew he was to be in Josefa's room at ten o'clock, you might have wanted him to have the illusion that he had—so to speak—a clear field. . . . (*She looks at him coldly*) It is only a suggestion. (*And then, finding a new place in his file*) When was the last time you used the Rolls-Royce limousine?

MADAME BEAUREVERS   The limousine? . . . Let me see—

JOSEFA (*Respectfully*)   The night before, Madame, for the gala . . .

MADAME BEAUREVERS   Ah, yes. My husband and I went to a diplomatic gala at the Opera.

JOSEFA   Madame wore a ballgown. Gray satin, with a train— (*Swishing it about in pantomime*)—she looked lovely in it. (SEVIGNE *looks puzzled, she goes on artlessly*) The next morning, even before I did the room, it had already been sent to the cleaners.

MADAME BEAUREVERS   A long skirt . . . someone probably stepped on it in the crush at the intermission.

JOSEFA   All afternoon—before the gala—Miguel was working on a leak in the crankcase of the limousine. The floor of the garage was covered with grease. And he didn't finish in time to clean it up.

SEVIGNE   Who does your cleaning, Madame?

MADAME BEAUREVERS (*Reluctantly*)   I—I have the name written down at home—

JOSEFA (*Cheerfully*)   Lacoste and Bergerie, Cleaners and Dyers, fifty-six avenue Victor Hugo. "Clothes Dyed Black for Mourning in 24 Hours." Madame.

SEVIGNE   Was there grease on the skirt of your ballgown, Madame?

MADAME BEAUREVERS   I—I did go to the garage that night . . . after we returned from the gala . . . I realized that I had left my gloves in the car . . . forgot them . . .

SEVIGNE Did you find them?

MADAME BEAUREVERS Yes.

SEVIGNE Where?

MADAME BEAUREVERS In the glove compartment, where I had put them. That's what a glove compartment is for, isn't it?

SEVIGNE (*Mildly*) In this particular glove compartment there also happened to be a fully loaded revolver.

MADAME BEAUREVERS No. It was no longer there.

SEVIGNE I see. Did you mention the disappearance of this weapon?

MADAME BEAUREVERS As a matter of fact, I did. I asked Miguel in the morning and he told me that my husband had taken it. There was no longer any need to keep it in the car, he said, and he would return it to the bank.

SEVIGNE It would help if this could be verified, but Ostos, unfortunately, is dead.

MADAME BEAUREVERS (*Coolly*) We all have to go when our time comes.

SEVIGNE At any rate, you found your gloves, so the trip to the garage was not a total loss.

JOSEFA And they were such beautiful, long gloves, buttoning up to the elbow—not the kind that are easy to put on and take off.

MADAME BEAUREVERS Well, I did. They were tight and uncomfortable—and I wanted to smoke.

SEVIGNE Sitting with your husband, in the back seat of the limousine—and you put your gloves in the compartment—*up front?*

(*There is unmistakably the feeling that* SEVIGNE *has sprung the trap.* MORESTAN, JOSEFA, *and* SEVIGNE *himself are all poised for the "kill"*)

MADAME BEAUREVERS We gave some friends a lift home in the car. There were six of us in all. My husband and I both sat in front. Ask him. He will confirm it.

(SEVIGNE *is pained, and except for* MADAME BEAUREVERS *there is general deflation*)

SEVIGNE Touché!

MADAME BEAUREVERS (*Relentlessly*) I am telling the truth. When I entered the room Ostos was dead, and my husband was kneeling beside your charming assistant—(*Indicating* JOSEFA)—naked as a plucked chicken, in a faint.

JOSEFA The traffic in my room that night! (*Tugging at her skirt*) Like the Place de la Concorde!

SEVIGNE Are you quite sure, Madame, that you mentioned the disappearance of the gun to Ostos?

MADAME BEAUREVERS Oh, yes, I remember it clearly.

SEVIGNE Since you did not then know *who* had taken the weapon, why did you not speak of it to your husband?

MADAME BEAUREVERS I meant to, in fact, but when I woke up the next morning he had already gone to the bank.

(JOSEFA *is gesturing frantically to the clock*)

SEVIGNE What time did you wake up, Madame?

MADAME BEAUREVERS Let me see . . . I think—

JOSEFA (*Respectfully*)   Madame rang for her coffee at noon.
(MADAME BEAUREVERS *turns to look at her, then back to* SEVIGNE)

SEVIGNE   Is that correct?

MADAME BEAUREVERS   Yes. I think so.
(JOSEFA *instantly pantomimes furiously "driving," with steering wheel, and horn-honking*)

SEVIGNE   At noon, Madame, Ostos had already left for Lyons.
(MORESTAN *stiffens,* JOSEFA *is tense with anticipation*)

MADAME BEAUREVERS   I sent for Ostos *before* I rang for my coffee. I woke up at eleven and when I rang, it was the cook who answered. I told her I wanted to see the chauffeur, and *then* to send Josefa with my coffee. (*Turning to* JOSEFA) I didn't ring that morning, did I, Josefa? It was the cook who told you to take up my tray, wasn't it?

JOSEFA (*Reluctantly*)   Yes, Madame.
(*She is let down, as are they all, except for* MADAME BEAUREVERS)

MADAME BEAUREVERS   You see, I am telling the truth. I took it for granted that my husband had taken the revolver from the car. He knew Ostos was maniacally jealous and even though he had planned to get him out of the way while he frolicked in the maid's room, I daresay it seemed wise not to leave a loaded gun where Ostos could get at it. That is certainly plausible, is it not?

SEVIGNE   It would appear to be . . .

MADAME BEAUREVERS   Oh, I don't think he *meant* to kill Ostos, particularly since his date with Josefa was for eleven o'clock and he didn't believe that Ostos could conceivably get back until long after midnight. But—(*With a shrug*) Ostos did manage to return soon after eleven, in time to find them together, and—you know what happened then.

SEVIGNE Not an unlikely reconstruction, I must admit—(JOSEFA *is rocking with pain*) How did you know your husband had arranged to meet Josefa at eleven o'clock that night, Madame?

MADAME BEAUREVERS (*Uncertain*) What do you mean?

SEVIGNE I mean, how did you know that the rendezvous was to be at eleven o'clock that night?

MADAME BEAUREVERS I didn't know. *You* told me. You asked me about a note he sent.

SEVIGNE True, I did. But I said *ten o'clock*. (MADAME BEAUREVERS *is suddenly tense and alert*) I mentioned the note twice, Madame, and each time—deliberately, I must admit—I said the date was for ten. But you knew the exact hour, didn't you, Madame?

MADAME BEAUREVERS (*A touch of hoarseness now*) It's not true. You said eleven. You must have said that.

SEVIGNE Morestan! Quickly—your notes!
(MORESTAN *flips back a few pages. Even he is animated*)

MORESTAN (*Reading*) "On the day of the shooting, in the afternoon, your husband sent Josefa a note fixing a rendezvous for ten o'clock that night . . ." (*Looking up from his notes*) And here again—(*Reading*) "—if you had intercepted your husband's note and knew that he was to be in Josefa's room—at ten o'clock."

MADAME BEAUREVERS (*Wildly*) No! No!

SEVIGNE Then how did you know the time that was in the note? Answer, Madame! It's crucial now because you are challenged by your own words—not mine or your husband's or any other witness's—your own. How did you know the time of the meeting? How?

MADAME BEAUREVERS (*Weakly*) I—I got the note. . . .
(SEVIGNE *nods, with no particular elation*)

SEVIGNE And the rest of it? . . .

MADAME BEAUREVERS (*Stubbornly*) No! . . . No! . . . I deny it!
(SEVIGNE *sighs heavily. Waits a moment in which* MAD-AME BEAUREVERS *stares at him, then shifts her gaze uneasily. He goes to the door, opens it, beckons*)

SEVIGNE You, there—Guard!
(*The* GUARD *looms up behind him*)

MADAME BEAUREVERS (*Almost a whisper*) You're arresting me?

SEVIGNE You should have time to think, Madame. (*Crosses to adjoining room, holds the door open*) The affair can conceivably be regarded as a crime of passion, prompted by your husband's misconduct. Your lawyers will undoubtedly give you that advice.

MADAME BEAUREVERS And you?

SEVIGNE (*Wearily*) I am not a judge, Madame, only a magistrate. (*She rises finally, quite proud and erect. She goes to the open door and* SEVIGNE *gestures to the* GUARD *to follow*) Madame is not to be left alone.
(*She pauses in the doorway to give him an appraising look*)

MADAME BEAUREVERS Don't worry about my attempting suicide; I am not quite so obliging.

(*The* GUARD *follows her in, the door closes*)

JOSEFA (*Admiringly*) They've got class, eh? My God, if I had killed somebody I'd be trembling like a leaf. (*As an afterthought*) Especially if I got caught. (SEVIGNE *is slumped wearily behind his desk*) You were sensational! (*As* SEVIGNE *shrugs it off, she turns to* MORESTAN) He was brilliant, wasn't he?

MORESTAN Oh, yes—very.

(SEVIGNE *has written something on a pad, now tears it loose*)

SEVIGNE Here, Morestan, get this countersigned by the Chief Prosecutor.

MORESTAN (*Bleakly*) Right.

(*He takes the paper, starts out*)

SEVIGNE (*To* JOSEFA) That's an order for your release. When he brings it back, you're free.

JOSEFA (*Calling after* MORESTAN) Don't trip! (*As the door closes, to* SEVIGNE, *in a curious tone*) Free!

SEVIGNE Don't you like the idea?

JOSEFA Oh, sure. That damn prison! (*And then*) I'll *really* be free. The man who loved me is dead; the man I loved . . . (*Bitterly*) He thinks I'm some kind of marijuana bush. (*Wistfully*) And if that's not free enough, I'm also out of a job!

SEVIGNE You'll get something else.

JOSEFA Oh, sure! With a reference I can expect from Madame —cashier in a bank! (*Gives* SEVIGNE *a sunny, reassuring smile*) Don't worry—I've got plans.

SEVIGNE Good.

JOSEFA Strip tease. (*Ignoring his pained look, she rattles on cheerfully*) I heard about it in prison. Two of the girls in my cell told me. They said I could make two hundred francs a night, anywhere in Montmartre. These two made even more than that—probably why they were in prison—but they told me where to go, who to ask for—everything. (*Finally slowing down at* SEVIGNE's *reaction*) Oh? Don't you think it's a good idea?

SEVIGNE It's not really for me to say. . . .

JOSEFA Oh, come on, you know more about me than anybody else except Miguel—and Monsieur Beaurevers and—(*Embarrassed*)—well, a few people. (*As* SEVIGNE *smiles*) Very few.

SEVIGNE I don't think you're like the girls you met in prison . . .

JOSEFA (*Delighted*) No? Truly?

SEVIGNE Truly.

JOSEFA After all you've heard about me . . .

SEVIGNE After all I've heard.

JOSEFA (*Marveling*) A man like you—I mean, you're practically a Judge!

SEVIGNE (*Wryly*) Practically.

JOSEFA I don't know what to say. I'm bowled over. (*Warmly, eyes shining*) Would you like it if . . . you know, you and I . . . well, you know—(*Impulsively*) I mean, I like you, too. Otherwise, I wouldn't dream of it.

SEVIGNE (*Startled*) Josefa!

JOSEFA I know that I would have been in the soup if not for you . . . and I *do* like you . . . And, well, you know so much about me already, so if you know a little more . . . (*She shrugs, smiles*) So?

SEVIGNE (*Gently*) No. Thank you, Josefa, but no.

JOSEFA You're sure? I mean, I know it's not a sensational offer, or anything, but I don't have much—

SEVIGNE (*Earnestly*) It is. Don't ever let anyone tell you it isn't. I'm touched and pleased that you should offer it. . . . (*Smiling*) But no, Josefa.

JOSEFA All right. But, you've done so much—(*Suddenly, quite shyly*) Would you like it if I *didn't* do the strip tease?

SEVIGNE Yes—very much.

JOSEFA All right—(*Cheerfully*) In December—with those draughts—who needs it?

SEVIGNE Get a good job, meet a nice fellow, settle down.

JOSEFA A nice fellow! (*Doubtfully*) You think I'm good luck? (*As he nods*) I don't know. Nice fellows—you think they're all that easy to find? (*Her sunny smile flashes again*) Now, you're nice. . . . (*Appraisingly*) In a way, you know, it's a pity. . . .

SEVIGNE Yes, it is. Luckily, I'm old enough to say: "Thank you, no"—(*With a smile*)—but I'm young enough to regret it. (*Then, severely*) And you—keep your mind on a job, a nice fellow. That's an order.

JOSEFA Yes, sir.

(MORESTAN *enters, empty-handed, with a frustrated gesture. He looks as though he had been through a bad few minutes*)

SEVIGNE   What is it? Where's the release order?

MORESTAN   On the Chief Prosecutor's desk.

SEVIGNE   Didn't he sign it?
(JOSEFA *is looking from one to the other as at a tennis match*)

MORESTAN   Sign it? He wouldn't even look at it. (*He adds*) I think he's willing to release us—but not her.

SEVIGNE (*Grimly*)   I'll see about that.
(*He exits quickly*)

MORESTAN (*Sitting down*)   Whew! (*Mops his forehead*) Wait till he gets upstairs. The Chief's office is teeming with Judges, Deputies, Ministers, high officials—all related to the Beaurevers.

JOSEFA   Will he— Is he in trouble?

MORESTAN   Ha! (*Making it clear*) H-A, with an exclamation mark.

JOSEFA   Because he got me out of trouble! (*A wail*) Oh, no!

MORESTAN   Don't worry. The Chief has these sullen periods but they never last more than a few years.

JOSEFA   What will they do to him?

MORESTAN   Oh, he'll live . . . (*With a shrug*) Not as well, perhaps, as if he had followed orders . . .

JOSEFA   They won't make him a judge?

MORESTAN   A judge! Ha!! H-A, with two exclamation marks.

JOSEFA   It's my fault! Me and my stupid innocence! If I had any sense I'd be guilty and everyone would be better off!

(MORESTAN *sighs, as if this would be too good to be true.*
JOSEFA *is slumped miserably in her chair. The* GUARD
comes to the door of the adjoining room)

GUARD Monsieur!
(*The* GUARD *beckons to* MORESTAN, *who crosses to him.
The* GUARD *whispers something,* MORESTAN *nods bleakly.
The* GUARD *goes back in, the door closes.* MORESTAN *turns
to his desk, takes pencils and notebook*)

MORESTAN Madame wishes to make a statement. When he gets
back—if he gets back—tell him.
(MORESTAN *goes into the adjoining room.* JOSEFA *sits
down, and after a moment,* SEVIGNE *enters*)

SEVIGNE Where's Morestan?

JOSEFA Inside—with Madame. She wanted to make a statement.

SEVIGNE Yes, I thought she'd get around to that. Here is the
order for your release—signed.
(*He is surprised when* JOSEFA *retreats from him, her
hands behind her back*)

JOSEFA No! No, I don't want it!

SEVIGNE What's wrong with you?
(*He tries to force the paper on her, she retreats*)

JOSEFA No! I refuse! (*She has backed away as far as she can
go*) You're in trouble, because you got me out of trouble—

SEVIGNE That's none of your business!

JOSEFA It is! Send her home! *I'll* confess. (*He stops, looking
at her curiously*) I don't mind—honest.

SEVIGNE (*Curtly*) I do.

JOSEFA I was just putting on an act about the prison—it was fun, I liked it.

SEVIGNE (*Softly*) You damn fool!

JOSEFA All her relatives—presidents and prime ministers and deputies—why should you have all that lot on your hands? With me, even if they sent me to the guillotine, you wouldn't even get a complaint on a postcard.

SEVIGNE Stop that! (*She just looks at him*) Idiot!

JOSEFA I know. I am. (*Eagerly*) I'll get into some trouble anyway—see if I don't. I'd much rather give you a nice confession. You'll get promoted—

SEVIGNE Who's been telling you all this? Was it Morestan?

JOSEFA No—(*Weakly*)—I guessed.

SEVIGNE Now, listen: You owe me nothing. They gave me this shabby little room and a handful of puzzle pieces. And then the machinery worked—properly, for once—and it got put together. You just happened to be one of the pieces. (*With a smile*) I'm glad of that.

JOSEFA I'm glad you were running the machine. (*And then, a wail*) But I want you to be a judge!

SEVIGNE I'll make it. Promise! (*He gives her the release order, she takes it reluctantly*) I'll have someone see you out with this—(*Indicating the document, he goes to the entrance door, opens it, beckons*) Guard!

JOSEFA So . . . it's finished?

SEVIGNE Finished.

JOSEFA Oh, well . . .
　　　　(*She looks him up and down in a lingering way*)

SEVIGNE (*Sternly*) Josefa!

JOSEFA Sorry . . . (*Apologetically*) I wish I could give you something—a souvenir. (*She smiles delightedly, shaking loose the square of silk crumpled in her hand, and extending it to him shyly*) Please. It's nothing, but it would be a keepsake . . . See—it's from the bullfights—the matador, and the bull, and everything. Miguel brought it to me last year from Bayonne. (*Urging it on him*) Please!

SEVIGNE All right. Thank you, Josefa. Thank you very much.

JOSEFA It's nothing.
(*They shake hands, and* SEVIGNE *starts for the adjoining room, while she watches him; he turns and waves the silk handkerchief*)

SEVIGNE Ole! Ole!

JOSEFA Ole! Ole!

SEVIGNE Remember—a good job, a nice fellow—you'll know how to make him happy.

JOSEFA I hope I remember.
(JOSEFA *turns and exits slowly, while* SEVIGNE *watches her*)

Curtain